# TAO TE CHING

PHOTOGRAPHY BY JANE ENGLISH

CALLIGRAPHY BY GIA-FU FENG

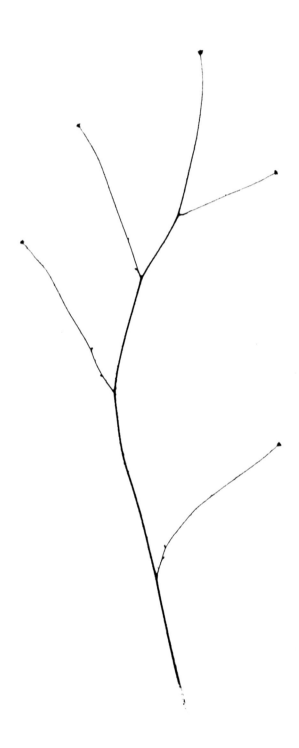

# TAO TE CHING

## Lao Tsu

TRANSLATED BY GIA-FU FENG AND JANE ENGLISH WITH TOINETTE LIPPE

INTRODUCTION BY JACOB NEEDLEMAN

VINTAGE BOOKS    A DIVISION OF PENGUIN RANDOM HOUSE LLC, NEW YORK

The Library of Congress has catalogued the original edition as follows:

Lao-tzŭ
Tao te ching
I Feng, Gia-fu, tr.  II English, Jane, tr.  III Title
[BL1900.L3 F46      1972b]      299'.51'482    72-2338

**Vintage Books Trade Paperback ISBN: 978-0-307-94930-1**
**eBook ISBN: 978-0-307-74544-6**

www.vintagebooks.com

Printed in Canada
13 12

# FOREWORD

This translation of the *Tao Te Ching* was one of the first books I edited at Alfred A. Knopf. I was sitting quietly in my office one day in October 1971 when the receptionist called to say that Gia-fu Feng and Jane English had arrived with a manuscript. There is one thing you learn very early on if you are an editor: Try to read part or all of a manuscript before you discuss it with the author. Otherwise there is little to talk about, since the author has read it but you have not. In this case, not only had I not read anything by these people, I didn't even know who they were. However, something stopped me from saying, "Tell them to leave the manuscript. I'm busy now. I'll be in touch when I've read it." I found myself walking out to greet them and returned to my office with a small Ho Chi Minh-like figure, complete with wispy beard, and his tall, strong American companion. I sat them down and asked them what had brought them to see me.

They told me that Macmillan, whose offices were across the street, had published Gia-fu Feng's first book *Tai Chi, a Way of Centering, and I Ching* but that his editor had left and the young man who had read the new manuscript and liked it would also be leaving at the end of the week. The young man told them that there was therefore no one at Macmillan with any enthusiasm for the book and he recommended that they show the manuscript to me. I was very taken aback. I had met this young editor a couple of times but did not think that he was aware that I practiced the ancient Chinese exercise of tai chi chuan. When I mentioned this to Gia-fu and Jane, they expressed surprise and delight. The editor at Macmillan had not known about this but had simply felt that I might be open to the possibility of publishing their new book, which was a translation of the *Tao Te Ching*. He was right. I sat and turned the pages in wonder. Each chapter was accompanied by Chinese calligraphy and an exquisite photograph or two. I persuaded them to leave the manuscript with me so that I could show it to the editor-in-chief. When I took it to him, he saw right away that the photos were magnificent but he pointed out that I knew nothing about publishing photographic books. I agreed with him but said that I had a hunch about this book. He believed me for some curious reason, I offered Gia-fu and Jane a contract, and I started work on the project immediately.

As I studied the translation, I realized that it had quite a way to go before it would measure up to the photographs. I consulted other translations and was astounded to discover that Lao Tsu's *Tao Te Ching* had been translated into English more often than any other book except the Bible. Still, the more versions I read, the more I realized how inaccessible many of them were. I don't read Chinese and could not compare any of them with the original. So I chose a dozen translations ranging from Arthur Waley's historically accurate version to Witter Bynner's lyrical poem, which seemed to take liberties with the text while perfectly expressing its spirit.

I would study how each of the twelve translators had rendered a particular sentence and then return to Gia-fu's translation to see what he thought it meant. Then I would find a way to express his understanding in a simple natural way and in words that had not been used by other translators. It was the opposite of plagiarism! Finally, I would read each page aloud to a young Mexican friend and if it did not read well or if she looked puzzled, I would adjust the words or the cadence until the meaning was clearly delivered. I then sent batches of the new text to Gia-fu who would approve (or occasionally disapprove) of what I had done. I have the suspicion that he thought that this was the normal editorial process, which it is not.

Eventually the time came to write jacket copy for the book. This is the moment every editor dreads because you have to find a way to express the essence of the work in a few sentences so that the reader will grasp immediately what the book has to offer. I was daunted at the prospect of reducing this classic from the sixth century B.C. to a single paragraph. Weeks went by and finally I had only twenty minutes left. I sat down at the typewriter and my mind went blank (not deliberately). I waited a little while and then began to type. I was amazed at what appeared on the page, and after all these years I am still amazed:

Accept what is in front of you without wanting the situation to be other than it is. Study the natural order of things and work with it rather than against it, for to try to change what *is* only sets up resistance. Nature provides everything without requiring payment or thanks. It does so without discrimination. So let us present the same face to everyone and treat them all as equals, however they may behave. If we watch carefully, we will see that work proceeds more quickly and easily if we stop "trying," if we stop making an extra effort, if we stop looking for results. In the clarity of a still and open mind, truth will be reflected. We will come to appreciate the original meaning of the word "understand," which means "stand under." We need to serve whatever or whoever stands before us, without any thought for ourselves. *Te*—which may be translated as "virtue" or "strength"—lies always in *Tao,* meaning "the way" or "natural law." In other words: Simply be.

The rest is history (recent history). The book was very well received and friends would often recommend it to me as something I might like or tell me how it was the one book they had taken with them to a cabin in the mountains. My name was not in the book and they had no idea that I had been its midwife, so I would smile and say that I was familiar with the book and felt that way too. Perhaps the final word came from *Time* magazine, where it was described as "the *Tao Te Ching* gussied up with photographs." As I said to the reviewer, who came to work at Knopf many years later, "What you wrote is true, but until it was gussied up with photographs, the *Tao Te Ching* had been around for twenty-five hundred years and *Time* magazine hadn't bothered to review it." And now, in 2011, it has sold more copies than any other English translation—more than a million copies in North America—and continues to sell several hundred a week.

It wasn't until a couple of years ago, when I read Carol Ann Wilson's book *Still Point of the Turning World*, the biography of Gia-fu Feng, who died in 1985, that I learned how Gia-fu and Jane's translation came into being. Gia-fu owned both ancient and modern Chinese versions of the *Tao Te Ching* and, to begin with, he translated both versions character by character and compared the two. He then shared one chapter each day with the students of the Stillpoint community, which he had founded five years earlier. Each morning the group studied the text as a spiritual exercise, exploring its ideas and refining the language, and Jane made sure that Gia-fu's "Chinese" English was transformed into standard American English.

By the time the chapters were typed up, the idea of a book in which the translation was enhanced with photographs and calligraphy had taken hold. This seemed obvious to both Gia-fu and Jane. Jane remembers that even before she met Gia-fu, "I would think of my photographs as Chinese landscape paintings and imagined where the calligraphy would go. In my photographing I was intuitively going around and beyond words and seeing the ineffable, sometimes called Tao, through nature. I especially delighted in creating photographs that teetered on the boundary between being and non-being—tree branches that delicately merge with the sky, fog almost obscuring a mountain, details of shells or grass that are almost unrecognizable. All this was for me a way to go beyond the too static 'thingness' of ordinary consciousness, a doorway to a vastness that seemed to be my native land."

So Jane set up a darkroom in the basement, where she worked on the photos and the layout, while in another room Gia-fu took up his brush and wrote page after page of elegant calligraphy which he had learned as a child from an eminent classical scholar in Shanghai.

In 1989 we decided that a smaller format (without the photographs and calligraphy) would be easier for people to carry around with them and so we published a study edition with an introduction, notes, and a bibliography by Jacob Needleman.

Over time all languages shift and some words and phrases become less immediate than they were a generation or so earlier. It is almost forty years since I worked on this translation, and the English language has changed in many ways. Jane English and I have stayed in touch ever since she and Gia-fu arrived in my office with the manuscript, and in the summer of 2010 she asked me to help her refresh and renew the translation with an eye to eliminating gender-specific language and other infelicities. In the 1970s we were still using *man* and *he* when referring to each member of the human race. Until the middle of the twentieth century the Chinese did not use pronouns (classical Chinese did not indicate gender, number, case, tense, or mood, all of which were inferred from the context) and Jane felt that it would be good to hew closer to this than we had done in the first edition and find alternatives to the sexist language. Jane English, Carol Wilson, Jacob Needleman, and I took a long clear look at the translation to see where we needed to adjust a word or a phrase. The result is this new edition which remains faithful to the original text while using contemporary language that rings true for our time. In addition, Jane has replaced more than half of the original photographs with others that she has made in the ensuing years.

When the twenty-fifth-anniversary edition of the book was published in 1997, Jane invited me to include the story of its publication (which I have recounted above). She wrote in her preface: "Like the sage in the *Tao Te Ching* who 'works without recognition' (Ch. 77), Toinette was an integral, but not mentioned, part of the creation of this book." This time around, as we worked on the "re-vision" of the text, Jane asked me to expand the story into a foreword to the new edition and show how the Tao had been at work in the very publication of the book. She also said to me that she felt that the translation was really "your baby" and that she wanted to add my name to hers and Gia-fu's as one of the translators of the book. This is a great honor and I offer her a deep bow.

I suggested that we should include something about how the book, and the Tao itself, changed the lives of each of the three of us—Gia-fu, Jane, and me.

*Gia-fu:* Since Gia-fu is no longer alive, I consulted with his biographer, Carol Wilson, who never met him but who went to great lengths to discover whatever she could about his life both in China and America. She told me that the book's publication probably had a twofold effect. One was the gratification he felt for the success of a Chinese classic he so loved, which strengthened his sense of self and what he could contribute to the world. Second, it seemed to catapult Gia-fu onto a larger stage. It gave him increased name recognition and credibility. The workshops he began to conduct throughout Europe, the United States, and Australia, were a direct result of the book's success. The substance of the workshops was what he had been doing at Stillpoint—tai chi chuan, calligraphy, and encounter/group therapy/community work. He didn't change direction in any dramatic way. What happened was that, more than any other single event in his life, the book's success deepened and enhanced what he was already doing.

*Jane:* My first answer to the question of how the publication of the *Tao Te Ching* that I created in 1971 with my late husband Gia-fu Feng has changed my life would be, "It influenced everything." As this new edition is published in the fall of 2011, I am sixty-nine years old, and the forty years the book has existed is considerably more than half my life. I find it hard to remember "life before Tao." Its wisdom and its mystery have seeped into my being. Or maybe more accurately, it has given me access to my own innate wisdom and sense of mystery.

One obvious effect has been a modest but steady source of income that has allowed me the freedom to follow my creativity wherever it led me, without the constraint of having to work at a regular job. Then there is the ongoing affirmation of the value of my photography to others—the delight people find in seeing my black-and-white photographs of nature. Appreciative emails come to me regularly, often with stories of how the book has influenced that person's life.

This appreciation of my work led me to ask a friend who owns a bookstore if she thought a wall calendar based on the book would be a good idea. She paused a moment, then said with a smile, "What took you so long?" So in 1991 I began creating the annual Tao calendar. Initially it included only photographs that had appeared in the book, but, later on, photographs I made in the years after the book's publication were included.

Also, there are the people I have met over the years because of the book—such a variety from around the world. Particularly delightful are the times when, in some other context, such as in the late 1990s, when I piloted a hot-air balloon commercially, people would suddenly look at me and say things like, "You're *the* Jane English! I have had your *Tao Te Ching* for years." Many good laughs come from moments like this.

I often find myself filled with gratitude and wonder at all that the *Tao Te Ching* has brought my way.

*Toinette:* Once the book was published, friends and family started giving me brushes, sticks of ink, ink stones, "rice" paper, and books on Chinese art, saying that they believed I would enjoy brush painting. I had no art training nor any inclination to follow their advice, so I shrugged, put everything on a shelf, and ignored it for years. In 2000, on the day my son started work, I felt that I had paid my dues to society and I quit my full-time job at Knopf. Until that moment, work had consumed me and I wanted to discover how to play, something that had eluded me for far too long. About six months later I found myself lingering outside a small sumi-e school in Soho (New York City) and a few weeks after that I started my apprenticeship there.

Learning the time-honored craft of East Asian brush painting has been a long and thorny road. It took me six years to see that the greatest obstacle I faced was that I had spent my life trying to control the outcome of everything I did. But art is uncontrollable. The muse is not on call. Each day it is necessary for me to be here, brush in hand, in case this is the day she decides to visit. What I'm hoping is that one day my "works on paper" will be transformed into "plays on paper." The spontaneous style of East Asian brush painting that I practice—and now teach—seeks to express the essence of whatever it is with a few swift and daring strokes. Ancient Chinese masters described it as allowing "the brush to dance and the ink to sing." Now I yearn to experience wonder, joy, and delight as I paint and to express these qualities in such a way that others may experience them too. And I realize that immersing myself in the Tao these many years has led me to abandon my love affair with words and opened my eyes to the miracle of the natural world around us.

Some months ago I decided it would be good to choose the music and readings for my own memorial service, so that whoever was around to cope when the moment arrived wouldn't have so much to do. Selecting the music wasn't hard, but the words… Eventually it came to me that the jacket copy for the *Tao Te Ching* I had written back in 1972, distilling the wisdom of this great classic, described the way in which I had tried to live my life and, if I hadn't always succeeded, it wasn't for lack of trying (something I would like mentioned at the service). The Tao truly does work in extraordinary ways.

— Toinette Lippe

# Introduction

The eighty-one short chapters known as the *Tao Te Ching* have been translated into English more often than any other book except the Bible, which is to say that its appeal is as broad as its meaning is deep. It speaks to each of us at our own level of understanding, while inviting us to search for insight and experience that are not yet within our comprehension. As with every text that deserves to be called sacred, it is a half-silvered mirror. To read it is not only to see ourselves as we are but to glimpse a greatness extending far beyond our knowledge of ourselves and the universe we live in.

"The Tao that can be told is not the eternal Tao": These words are among the most famous in all world literature. They were first offered, however, some 2,500 years ago, not to modern Western people like ourselves, but to a people and in a place, ancient China, far removed from us. Any work of art that communicates so enduringly over such enormous reaches of time and cultural diversity addresses, we may be sure, the essence of human nature and the human condition, rather than sociocultural aspects that are peculiar to this or that society. The *Tao Te Ching* deals with what is permanent in us. It speaks of a possible inner greatness and an equally possible inner failure, which are both indelibly written into our very structure as human beings. Under its gaze, we are not "American" or "Chinese" or "European." We are human beings, uniquely called to occupy a specific place in the cosmic order, no matter where or in what era we live.

The *Tao Te Ching* is thus a work of metaphysical psychology, taking us far beyond the social or biological factors that have been the main concern of modern psychology. It helps us see how the fundamental forces of the cosmos itself are mirrored in our own individual, inner structure. And it invites us to try to live in direct relationship to all these forces. To see truly and to live fully: this is what it means to be authentically human. But it is extremely challenging, and this challenge was apparently as difficult for the men and women of ancient China as it is for us. We too try in vain to live full lives without understanding what it means to *see*. We, too, presume to act, to do, to create, without opening ourselves to a vision of ultimate reality. This opening and the way to experience it are what the *Tao Te Ching* is about.

Historical information about the text and its author is scant and cloaked in legend. Even the little information we have is at every point subject to dispute by scholars, although many are willing to accept that Lao Tsu was a real person born in what is now known as Henan province in China some six centuries before the Christian era. Tradition has it that Confucius once journeyed to see Lao Tsu and came away amazed and in awe of the man. According to the tale, Confucius described his meeting with Lao Tsu in the following way: "I know a bird can fly, a fish can swim, an animal can run. For that which runs a net can be made; for that which swims a line can be made; for that which flies a corded arrow can be made. But the dragon's ascent into heaven on the wind and the clouds is something which is beyond my knowledge. Today I have seen Lao Tsu who is perhaps like a dragon." [1]

The tale also tells that Lao Tsu was the keeper of the imperial archives at the ancient capital of Luoyang. Seeing the imminent decay of the society he lived in, he resolved to ride away alone into the desert. But at Hangu Pass he was stopped by a gatekeeper named Yin Xi, who knew of his reputation for wisdom and who begged him to set down in writing the essence of his teaching. Thus, legend tells us, the *Tao Te Ching* came into being.

Legend aside, there is no doubt about the immense importance of this text in the history of China and East Asia. The figure of Lao Tsu and his writings are revered by followers of the Taoist religion, and the message of the *Tao Te Ching* has been one of the major underlying influences in Chinese thought and culture for more than two thousand years. Throughout the world, when one thinks of the greatest spiritual figures in history, Lao Tsu is placed alongside Christ, the Buddha, Moses, and Muhammad.

Some remarks about the language of this work may be of help at this point. The word *Tao* (pronounced "dow") has been characterized as untranslatable by nearly every modern scholar. But this statement should not lead us to imagine that the meaning of the Tao was any more easily understood by the contemporaries of Lao Tsu. It would be more to the point to say, only half jokingly, that the word *Tao*, and even the whole of the *Tao Te Ching*, is not readily translatable into any language, including Chinese! "My words are easy to understand and easy to perform," wrote Lao Tsu, "Yet no one under heaven knows them or practices them" (Ch. 70).

The present translation generally leaves the word *Tao* in Chinese. Those who have sought an equivalent in Western languages have almost invariably settled on *Way* or *Path*. Metaphysically, the term *Tao* refers to the way things are; psychologically, it refers to the way human nature is constituted, the deep, dynamic structure of our being; ethically, it means the way human beings must conduct themselves with others; spiritually, it refers to the guidance that is offered to us, the methods of searching for the truth that have been handed down by the great sages of the past — the way of inner work. Yet all these meanings of *Tao* are ultimately one. In this work we are offered a vision that relates the flowing structure of the universe to

---

[1] Quoted D. C. Lau, *Tao Te Ching* (Harmondsworth, England: Penguin Books, 1963), 8.

the structure of our individual nature, both in itself and as it manifests in the details of our everyday actions in the world.

No linguistic or philosophic analysis of this word can ever capture its essential meaning, because what is being referred to is an experience that can be understood only at the moment it is "tasted" with the whole of our being — simultaneously sensed, felt, and thought; and because this way of experiencing is entirely different from the way almost all of us act and think and feel in our usual lives.

To say that the realization of metaphysical truth lies in the opposite direction from the way we usually experience our lives is not to say that a different "method" of thinking or experiencing is required. What is at issue is nothing less than the activation of an entirely new power within us, an entirely new movement of consciousness. The point is that we are built to receive, contain, and transform this power and then to make our life a complete expression of it. Nothing else can bring us ultimate fulfillment. And yet our lives are lived with little awareness or contact with this force of consciousness. We work, we love, we struggle, we eat, sleep, and dream, we write books and create art, we even worship our gods closed off from it. This is why every sacred teaching in the history of the world begins as a revolution — incomprehensible, paradoxical, mysterious. Whether it be the gnomic teaching of Lao Tsu — whoever he was and *if* he was — or the profoundly troubling doctrine of unknowing brought by Socrates, or the exalted, hidden God speaking through Moses and the prophets of Israel, or the shattering sacrifice of love transmitted by Jesus, every sacred teaching remains sacred only as long as it opens a path that has never before been opened and yet always exists and must always exist for humanity.


Look, it cannot be seen — it is beyond form.

Listen, it cannot be heard — it is beyond sound.

Grasp, it cannot be held — it is intangible.

. . .

It is called indefinable and beyond imagination.

Stand before it and there is no beginning.

Follow it and there is no end.

Stay with the ancient Tao,

Move with the present.

(Ch. 14)

Of equal importance in approaching this text, and the life it calls us to, is the word *Te* (pronounced "deh"). This word directs our attention to the question of the expression or manifestation of the supreme reality in our day-to-day lives. The present text, following numerous other translations, renders *Te* by the English word *Virtue*. But we must be careful not to bring our ordinary moralistic associations to this term. It is true that the word *Te* introduces us to the ethical dimension of this teaching, but this is ethics that is solidly rooted in metaphysics, and completely separate from ethics considered as the rules of social morality, which vary from culture to culture, epoch to epoch, nation to nation, class to class. *Te* refers to nothing less than the quality of human action that allows the central, creative power of the universe to manifest through it.

Something mysteriously formed,

Born before heaven and earth.

In the silence and the void,

Standing alone and unchanging,

Ever present and in motion.

Perhaps it is the mother of ten thousand things.

I do not know its name.

Call it Tao.

For lack of a better word, I call it great.

Being great, it flows.

It flows far away.

Having gone far, it returns.

Therefore, "Tao is great;

Heaven is great;

Earth is great;

The human being is also great."

These are the four great powers of the universe,

And the human being is one of them.

The human being follows the earth.

Earth follows heaven.

Heaven follows the Tao.

Tao follows what is natural.

(Ch. 25)

The picture before us is of a cosmic force or principle that expands or flows outward or, more precisely perhaps, descends into the creation of the universe, "the ten thousand things." Together with this, we are told of a force or movement of return. All of creation returns to the source. But the initial coming-into-being of creation is to be understood as a receiving of that which flows downward and outward from the center. Every created entity ultimately is what it is and does what it does due to its specific reception of the energy radiating from the ultimate, formless reality. This movement from the nameless source to the ten thousand things is *Te*. Human beings are created to receive this force consciously and are called to allow their actions to manifest that force. Such conscious receiving in human life is Virtue. Thus, the movement that leads back to the source is also the opening toward great action in outer life. Virtue is an opening rather than a "doing."

In sum, Lao Tsu distinguished human Virtue from what we ordinarily consider moral action by the cosmic nature of the force that human Virtue manifests. Great action, for Lao Tsu, is action that conducts the highest and subtlest conscious energy. Ordinary moral action is, on the contrary, a manifestation whose source is "lower down" in the vast chain of being as it is portrayed in chapter 25: Tao, heaven, earth, the human being. The ego, our ordinary "initiator of action," is an ephemeral construction, which is formed by factors operating far beneath the level of the source and which, in the unenlightened state of awareness, represents a kind of blockage or impediment to the interplay of fundamental cosmic forces. In other words, because of our identification of ourselves with the ego, what we ordinarily call action, or "doing," cuts us off from the complete reception of conscious energy in our bodies and actions.

This idea must inevitably sound revolutionary, overthrowing the value we place on socially constructed systems of morality and efficiency. For the point is not only *what* we do but the source from which we do it. The metaphysical nature of that source determines the ethical, cognitive, and pragmatic value of all human action — that is, the goodness, truth, and practicality of what we do in our life on earth. Our primary and perhaps only true responsibility is to become individuals who are also conduits for the supreme creative power of the universe. All other responsibilities — for knowing the truth, for feeling the good, and for accomplishing what is useful and effective — must flow from this: in our external world, in our day-to-day lives, and within the recesses of our psychological makeup. In the ancient traditions of the West, this idea has been known as the doctrine of human being as microcosm. In Christian and Jewish mysticism, in the philosophy of Plato and the Hermetic tradition, in Islamic mysticism, we find this idea pouring forth in an endless symphony of symbolic forms and profoundly articulated ideas. In the *Tao Te Ching* it is offered to us as a whisper.

Thus:

Respect of Tao and honor of Virtue are not demanded,
But they are in the nature of things.

Therefore all things arise from Tao.
By Virtue they are nourished,
Developed, cared for,
Sheltered, comforted,
Grown, and protected.
Creating without claiming,
Doing without taking credit,
Guiding without interfering.
This is Primal Virtue.

(Ch. 51)

We are now in a position to consider what for many of us is the most compelling aspect of the *Tao Te Ching*, namely, the putting into practice of its teaching. The metaphysical doctrine now stands before us in outline: an unformed, ungraspable, pure conscious principle lies at the heart and origin of all things; it is referred to as the *Tao*. This principle moves, expands, descends into form, creating the hierarchically, organically ordered cascade of worlds and phenomena called "the ten thousand things," or simply the great universe — and this movement, especially as it can move through humanity, is called *Te*, Virtue. At the same time, there is a great tide of return to the source, back toward the undifferentiated, pure reality of the "uncarved block." This movement is also termed *Tao*. Finally, the supreme whole comprised of both movements is also given the designation *Tao*. (*Ching*, by the way, simply means "book.")

Each of us is built to be an individual incarnation of this whole. Our good, our happiness — the very meaning of our life — is to live in correspondence and relationship to the whole, to be and act precisely as the universe itself is and moves. The question before us now is *how?* The *Tao Te Ching* offers a powerful and practical answer, describing in almost every chapter this way of living, also known as *Tao*, the Way.

The secret of living, according to the *Tao Te Ching*, is to open within ourselves to the great flow of fundamental forces that constitute the ultimate nature of the universe both the movement that descends from the source *and* the movement of return.

Empty yourself of everything.

Let the mind become still.

The ten thousand things rise and fall while the self watches their return.

They grow and flourish and then return to the source.

Returning to the source is stillness, which is the way of nature.

(Ch. 16)

Expressions like this show us why the *Tao Te Ching* has assumed such great popularity. There is a widely shared realization that in our modern world we have arrogantly and foolishly believed in science, a product largely of the intellect alone and not of our whole being, as an instrument for imposing our will upon nature. And, in the relationships among peoples, Europeans and Americans have often assumed the right to impose their values and desires upon peoples whose lives are not yet based on the technological applications of science. As for Western religion, the Judeo-Christian tradition has sometimes been perceived, rightly or wrongly, as supporting this general tendency in the psychological sphere, especially insofar as it presents a fierce moral demand, a commandment that individuals override their own instinctive, emotional nature, and conform their lives to standards that suffocate the vital forces within the body and the heart of every human being.

There is nothing new in this reaction against what is perceived as the tyranny of an intellectualist and puritanical value system. Our culture heard it in the early criticism of the

Industrial Revolution — in the work of Blake, Dostoyevsky, Kierkegaard, and Nietzsche, to name only a few. The first half of the twentieth century saw aspects of it in the psychoanalytic movement, which sought to open our awareness to the forces of organic nature within us, and in the writings of the existentialists, who called for the recognition of a radical inner freedom unfixed and undetermined by any laws, cosmic or societal. Finally, in recent years we have witnessed the continually growing interest in mysticism and Eastern religion, which, despite some highly publicized bizarre concomitants, has introduced powerful new ideas into the currents of Western thought; chief among them, perhaps, is the idea of the states of human consciousness and the suggestion that our lives, individually and collectively, proceed in a diminished state of consciousness, far from what would be possible were we to live at the level of consciousness that is natural to us.

It is this last claim that can sound a truly new note for most people and that provides the context in which the *Tao Te Ching* can speak in a stunning, fresh way about the practical question of how to search for truth and how to live it. Once the immensity of the idea of levels of consciousness is felt, the message of the *Tao Te Ching* soars beyond social and philosophical criticism of our culture. We find ourselves in front of a teaching about nature and naturalness that compels us to see even our urgent concerns about the environment and our planet in a way that is far more immediate and at the same time far more inclusive than we might have imagined. And we shall see that the same holds true for other inescapable issues of our time, including the colossal problems of war and violence, the crisis of moral leadership, and the complexities of intimate human relationships.

—Jacob Needleman

# TAO TE CHING

道可道非常道名可名非常名無名天地之始

有名萬物之母故常無欲以觀其妙

常有欲以觀其徼此兩者同出而異名

同謂之元元之又元眾妙之門

## ONE

The Tao that can be told is not the eternal Tao.
The name that can be named is not the eternal name.
The nameless is the beginning of heaven and earth.
The named is the mother of ten thousand things.
Ever desireless, one can see the mystery.
Ever desiring, one can see the manifestations.
These two spring from the same source but differ in name;
This appears as darkness.
Darkness within darkness.
The gate to all mystery.

天下皆知美之為美斯惡已皆知善之為善斯不善已

故有無相生難易相成長短相較高下相傾音聲相和前後相隨

是以聖人處無為之事行不言之教萬物作焉而不辭

生而不有為而不恃功成而弗居

夫唯弗居是以不去

Two

Under heaven all can see beauty as beauty only because there is ugliness.
All can know good as good only because there is evil.

Therefore having and not having arise together;
Difficult and easy complement each other;
Long and short contrast each other;
High and low rest upon each other;
Voice and sound harmonize each other;
Front and back follow each other.

Therefore the wise go about doing nothing, teaching no-talking.
The ten thousand things rise and fall without cease,
Creating, yet not possessing,
Working, yet not taking credit.
Work is done, then forgotten.
Therefore it lasts forever.

THREE

Not exalting the gifted prevents quarreling.
Not collecting treasures prevents stealing.
Not seeing desirable things prevents confusion of the heart.

The wise therefore rule by emptying hearts and stuffing bellies,
By weakening ambitions and strengthening bones.
If people lack knowledge and desire,
Then it is best not to interfere.
If nothing is done, then all will be well.

不尚賢使民不爭不貴難得之貨使民不為盜

不見可欲使民心不亂

是以聖人之治虛其心實其腹弱其志強其骨

常使民無知無欲使夫智者不敢為也為無為則無不治

道沖而用之或不盈淵兮似萬物之宗挫其銳

解其紛和其光同其塵湛兮似或存

吾不知誰之子象帝之先

Four

The Tao is an empty vessel; it is used, but never filled.
Oh, unfathomable source of ten thousand things!
Blunt the sharpness,
Untangle the knot,
Soften the glare,
Merge with dust.
Oh, hidden deep but ever present!
I do not know from whence it comes.
It is the forefather of the ancestors.

天地不仁以萬物為芻狗聖人不仁以百姓為芻狗

天地之間其猶橐籥乎虛而不屈動而愈出

多言數窮不如守中

FIVE

Heaven and earth are impartial;
They see the ten thousand things as they are.
The wise are impartial;
They see the people as they are.

The space between heaven and earth is like a bellows.
The shape changes but not the form;
The more it moves, the more it yields.
More words count less.
Hold fast to the center.

谷神不死是謂元牝元牝之門是謂天地根

緜緜若存用之不勤

Six

The valley spirit never dies;
It is the woman, primal mother.
Her gateway is the root of heaven and earth.
It is like a veil barely seen.
Use it; it will never fail.

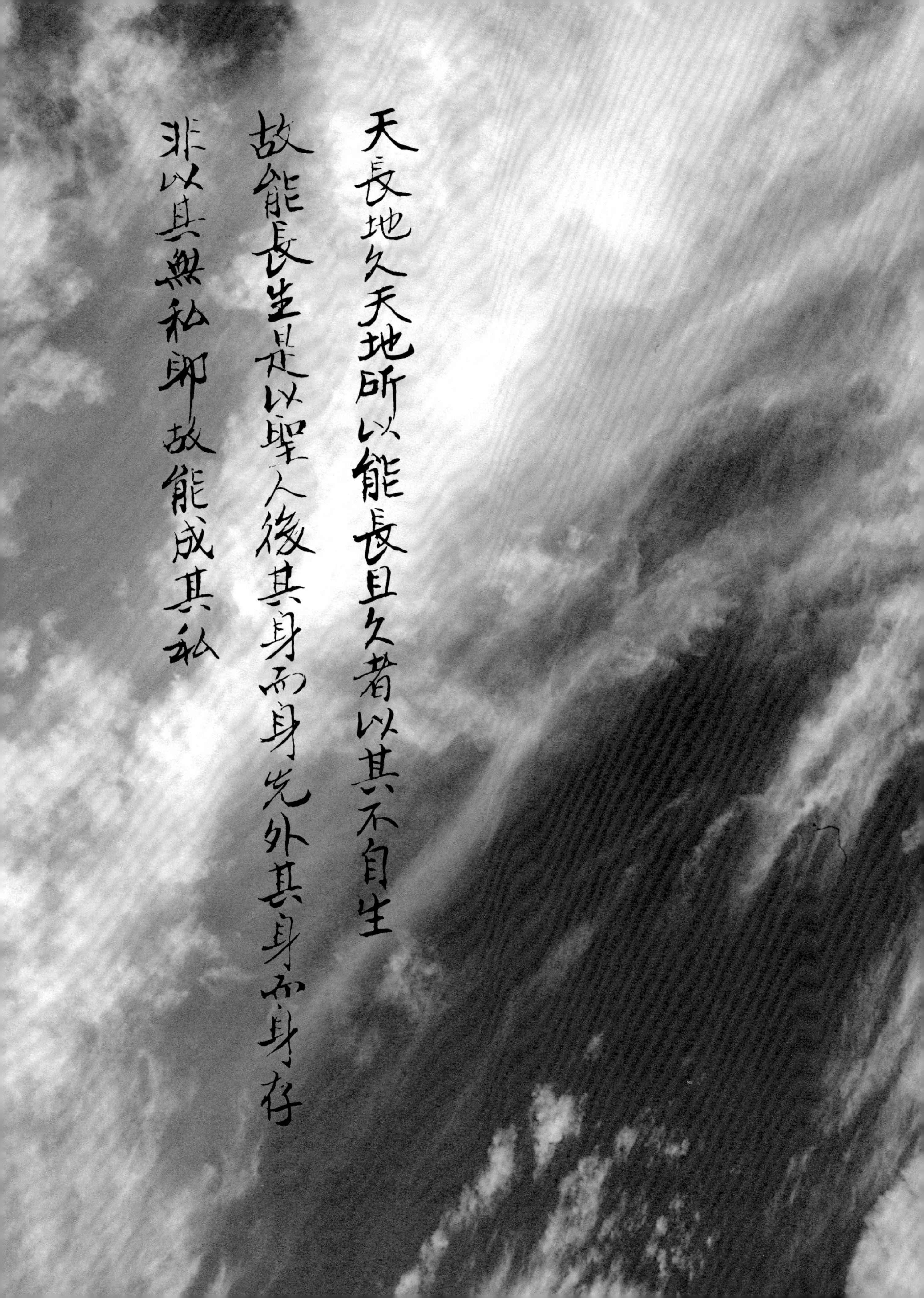

天長地久天地所以能長且久者以其不自生

故能長生是以聖人後其身而身先外其身而身存

非以其無私邪故能成其私

SEVEN

Heaven and earth last forever.
Why do heaven and earth last forever?
They are unborn,
So ever living.
The wise stay behind, and are thus ahead.
They are detached, thus at one with all.
Through selfless action, they attain fulfillment.

上善若水水善利萬物而不爭處眾人之所惡

故幾於道居善地心善淵與善仁言善信正善治

事善能動善時夫唯不爭故無尤

Eight

The highest good is like water.
Water gives life to the ten thousand things and does not strive.
It flows in places people reject and so is like the Tao.

In dwelling, be close to the land.
In meditation, go deep in the heart.
In dealing with others, be gentle and kind.
In speech, be true.
In ruling, be just.
In business, be competent.
In action, watch the timing.

No fight: No blame.

持而盈之不如其已揣而梲之不可長保

金玉滿堂莫之能守富貴而驕自遺其咎

功遂身退天之道

## Nine

Better stop short than fill to the brim.
Oversharpen the blade, and the edge will soon blunt.
Amass a store of gold and jade, and no one can protect it.
Claim wealth and titles, and disaster will follow.
Retire when the work is done.
This is the way of heaven.

載營魄抱一能無離乎專氣致柔能嬰兒乎
滌除元覽能無疵乎愛民治國能無知乎
天門開闔能無雌乎明白四達能無為乎
生之畜之生而不有為而不恃
長而不宰是謂元德

## Ten

Carrying body and soul and embracing the one,
Can you avoid separation?
Attending fully and becoming supple,
Can you be as a newborn babe?
Washing and cleansing the primal vision,
Can you be without stain?
Loving the people and ruling the country,
Can you be without cleverness?
Opening and closing the gates of heaven,
Can you play the role of woman?
Understanding and being open to all things,
Are you able to do nothing?
Giving birth and nourishing,
Bearing yet not possessing,
Working yet not taking credit,
Leading yet not dominating,
This is the Primal Virtue.

三十輻共一轂當其無有車之用

埏埴以為器當其無有器之用

鑿戶牖以為室當其無有室之用

故有之以為利無之以為用

Eleven

Thirty spokes share the wheel's hub;
It is the center hole that makes it useful.
Shape the clay into a vessel;
It is the space within that makes it useful.
Cut doors and windows for a room;
It is the holes that make it useful.
Therefore profit comes from what is there;
Usefulness from what is not there.

TWELVE

The five colors blind the eye.
The five tones deafen the ear.
The five flavors dull the taste.
Racing and hunting madden the mind,
Precious things lead us astray.

Therefore the wise are guided by what they feel and not by what they see,
Letting go of that and choosing this.

五色令人目盲五音令人耳聾五味令人口爽

馳騁畋獵令人心發狂難得之貨令人行妨

是以聖人為腹不為目

故去彼取此

寵辱若驚貴大患若身

何謂寵辱若驚寵為下得之若驚失之若驚是謂寵辱若驚

何謂貴大患若身吾所以有大患者為吾有身及吾無身吾有何患

故貴以身為天下若可寄天下愛以身為天下若可託天下

Thirteen

Accept disgrace willingly.
Accept misfortune as the human condition.

What do you mean by "Accept disgrace willingly"?
Accept being unimportant.
Do not be concerned with loss or gain.
This is called "accepting disgrace willingly."

What do you mean by "Accept misfortune as the human condition"?
Misfortune comes from having a body.
Without a body, how could there be misfortune?

Surrender yourself humbly; then you can be trusted to care for all things.
Love the world as your own self; then you can truly care for all things.

視之不見名曰夷聽之不聞名曰希搏之不得名曰微此三者不可致詰故混而為一其上不皦其下不昧

繩繩不可名復歸於無物是謂無狀之狀無物之象是謂惚恍

迎之不見其首隨之不見其後執古之道以御今之有能知古始是謂道紀

FOURTEEN

Look, it cannot be seen—it is beyond form.
Listen, it cannot be heard—it is beyond sound.
Grasp, it cannot be held—it is intangible.
These three are indefinable;
Therefore they are joined in one.

From above it is not bright;
From below it is not dark:
An unbroken thread beyond description.
It returns to nothingness.
The form of the formless,
The image of the imageless,
It is called indefinable and beyond imagination.

Stand before it and there is no beginning.
Follow it and there is no end.
Stay with the ancient Tao,
Move with the present.

Knowing the ancient beginning is the essence of Tao.

古之善為士者微妙元通深不可識

夫唯不可識故強為之容

豫焉若冬涉川猶兮若畏四鄰儼兮其若客

渙兮若冰之將釋敦兮其若樸曠兮其若谷

混兮其若濁孰能濁以靜之徐清孰能安以久動之徐生

保此道者不欲盈夫唯不盈故能蔽不新成

## Fifteen

The ancients were subtle, mysterious, profound, responsive.
The depth of their knowledge is unfathomable.
Because it is unfathomable,
All we can do is describe their appearance.
Watchful, as though crossing a winter stream.
Alert, like people aware of danger.
Courteous, like visiting guests.
Yielding, like ice about to melt.
Simple, like uncarved blocks of wood.
Hollow, like caves.
Opaque, like muddy pools.

Who can wait quietly while the mud settles?
Who can remain still until the moment of action?
Observers of the Tao do not seek fulfillment.
Not seeking fulfillment, they are not swayed by desire for change.

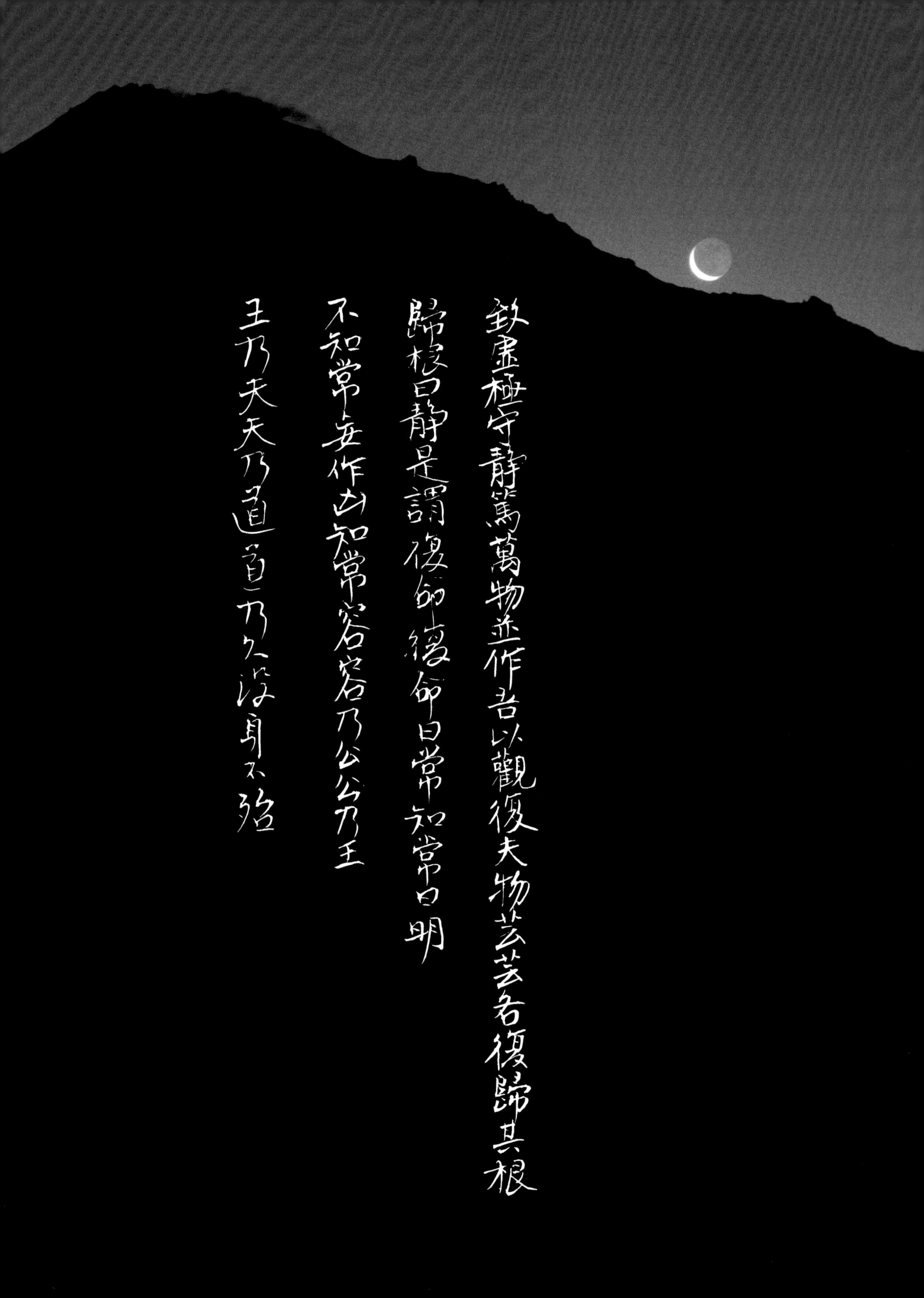

致虛極守靜篤萬物並作吾以觀復夫物芸芸各復歸其根

歸根曰靜是謂復命復命曰常知常曰明

不知常妄作凶知常容容乃公公乃王

王乃天天乃道道乃久沒身不殆

## Sixteen

Empty yourself of everything.
Let the mind become still.
The ten thousand things rise and fall while the self watches their return.
They grow and flourish and then return to the source.
Returning to the source is stillness, which is the way of nature.
The way of nature is unchanging.
Knowing constancy is insight.
Not knowing constancy leads to disaster.
Knowing constancy, the mind is open.
With an open mind, you will be openhearted.
Being openhearted, you will act royally.
Being royal, you will attain the divine.
Being divine, you will be at one with the Tao.
Being at one with the Tao is eternal.
And though the body dies, the Tao will never pass away.

太上下知有之其次親而譽之

其次畏之其次侮之

信不足焉有不信焉

悠兮其貴言功成事遂百姓皆謂我自然

Seventeen

Very few are aware of the highest.
Then comes that which they know and love,
Then that which is feared,
Then that which is despised.

Those who do not trust enough will not be trusted.

When actions are performed
Without unnecessary talk,
People say, "We did it!"

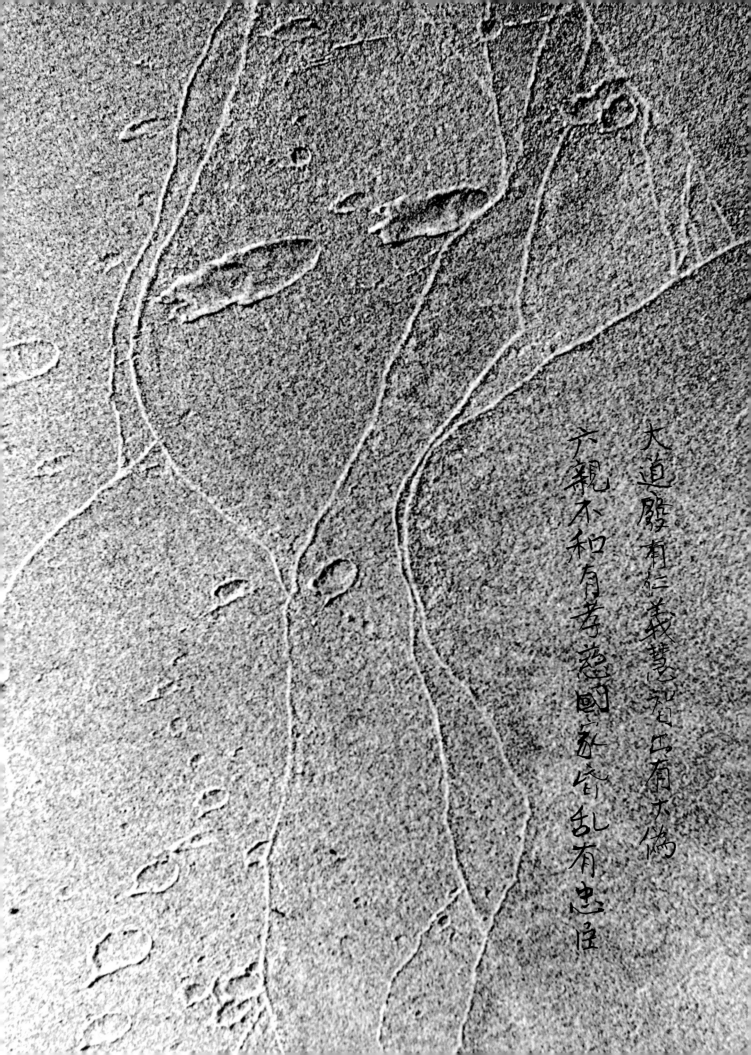

大道廢有仁義慧智出有大偽

六親不和有孝慈國家昏乱有忠臣

EIGHTEEN

When the great Tao is forgotten,
Kindness and morality arise.
When wisdom and intelligence are born,
The great pretense begins.

When there is no peace within the family,
Filial piety and devotion arise.
When the country is confused and in chaos.
Loyal ministers appear.

絕聖棄智民利百倍

絕仁棄義民復孝慈絕巧棄利盜賊無有

此三者以為文不足故令有所屬見素抱樸少私寡欲

Nineteen

Give up sainthood, renounce wisdom,
And it will be a hundred times better for everyone.

Give up kindness, renounce morality,
And people will rediscover filial piety and love.

Give up ingenuity, renounce profit,
And bandits and thieves will disappear.

These three are outward forms alone: They are not sufficient in themselves.
It is more important
To see the simplicity,
To realize our true nature,
To cast off selfishness
And temper desire.

絕學無憂　唯之與阿相去幾何　善之與惡相去若何

人之所畏不可不畏　荒兮其未央哉

眾人熙熙如享太牢　如春登臺我獨泊兮其未兆

如嬰兒之未孩　儽儽兮若無所歸　眾人皆有餘而我獨若遺

我愚人之心也哉　沌沌兮俗人昭昭我獨昏昏

俗人察察我獨悶悶　澹兮其若海　飂兮若無止

眾人皆有以而我獨頑似鄙　我獨異於人而貴食母

Twenty

Give up learning, and put an end to your troubles.

Is there a difference between yes and no?
Is there a difference between good and evil?
Must I fear what others fear? What nonsense!
Other people are contented, enjoying the sacrificial feast of the ox.
In spring some go to the park and climb the terrace,
But I alone am drifting, not knowing where I am.
Like a newborn babe before it learns to smile,
I am alone, without a place to go.

Others have more than they need, but I alone have nothing.
I am a fool. Oh, yes! I am confused.
Others are clear and bright,
But I alone am dim and weak.
Others are sharp and clever,
But I alone am dull and stupid.
Oh, I drift like the waves of the sea,
Without direction, like the restless wind.

Everyone else is busy,
But I alone am aimless and without desire.
I am different.
I am nourished by the great mother.

TWENTY-ONE

The greatest Virtue is to follow Tao and Tao alone.
The Tao is elusive and intangible.
Oh, it is intangible and elusive, and yet within is image.
Oh, it is elusive and intangible, and yet within is form.
Oh, it is dim and dark, and yet within is essence.
This essence is very real, and therein lies faith.
From the very beginning until now its name has never been forgotten.
Thus I perceive creation.
How do I know the ways of creation?
Because of this.

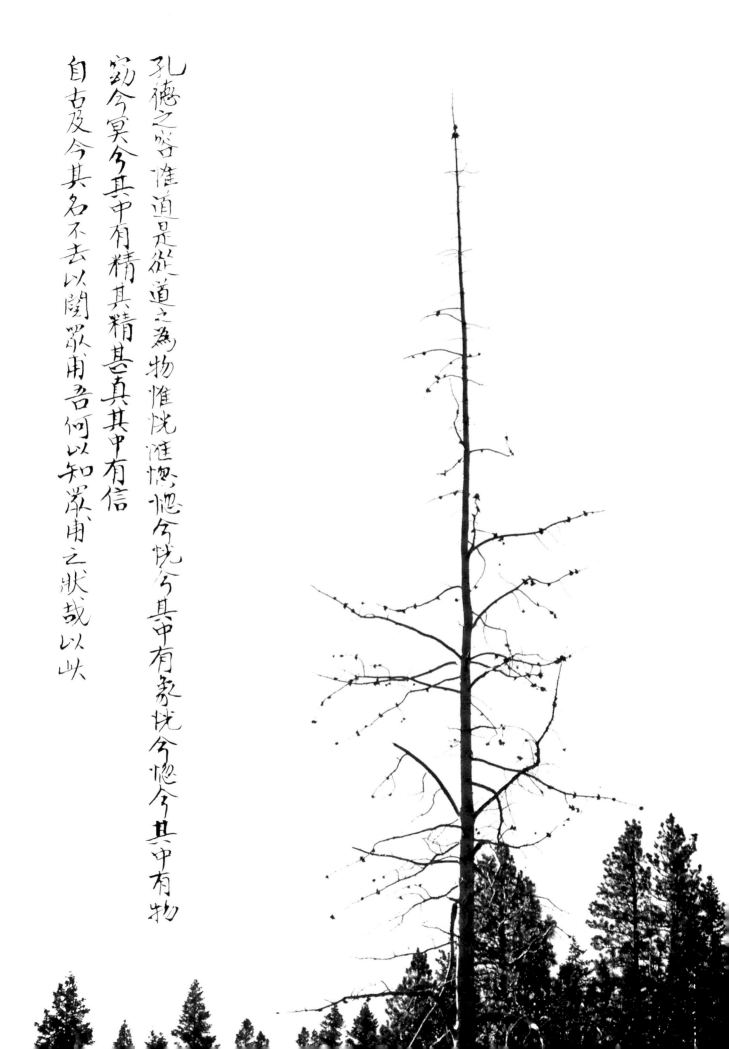

孔德之容惟道是從道之為物惟恍惟惚惚兮恍兮其中有象恍兮惚兮其中有物

窈兮冥兮其中有精其精甚真其中有信

自古及今其名不去以閱眾甫吾何以知眾甫之狀哉以此

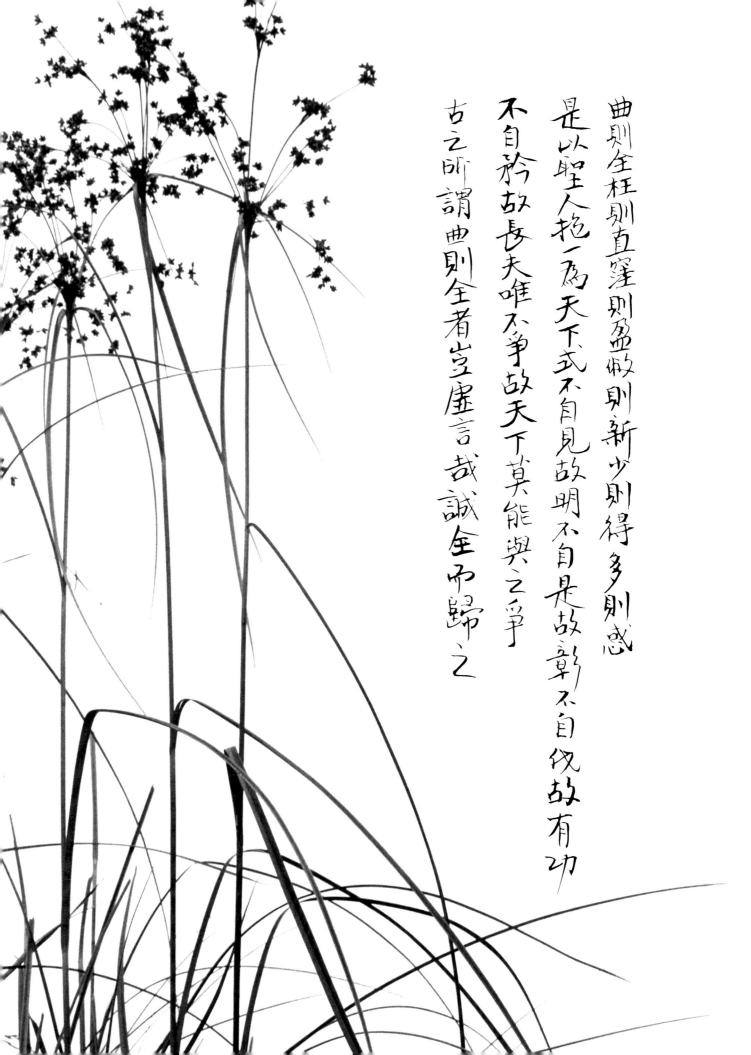

曲則全枉則直窪則盈敝則新少則得多則惑

是以聖人抱一為天下式不自見故明不自是故彰不自伐故有功

不自矜故長夫唯不爭故天下莫能與之爭

古之所謂曲則全者豈虛言哉誠全而歸之

TWENTY-TWO

Yield and overcome;
Bend and be straight;
Empty and be full;
Wear out and be new;
Have little and gain;
Have much and be confused.

Therefore the wise embrace the one
And set an example to all.
Not putting on a display,
They shine forth.
Not justifying themselves,
They are distinguished.
Not boasting,
They receive recognition.
Not bragging,
They never falter.
They do not quarrel,
So no one quarrels with them.
Therefore the ancients say, "Yield and overcome."
Is that an empty saying?
Be truly whole,
And all things will come to you.

Twenty-three

To talk little is natural.
High winds do not last all morning.
Heavy rain does not last all day.
Why is this? Heaven and earth!
If heaven and earth cannot make things last forever,
How is it possible for us?

Those who follow the Tao
Are at one with the Tao.
Those who are virtuous
Experience Virtue.
Those who lose their way
Are lost.
When you are at one with the Tao,
The Tao welcomes you.
When you are at one with Virtue,
Virtue is always there.
When you are at one with loss,
Loss is experienced willingly.

Those who do not trust enough
Will not be trusted.

希言自然故飄風不終朝驟雨不終日孰為此者天地

天地尚不能久而況於人乎

故從事於道者道者同於道德者同於德失者同於失

同於道者道亦樂得之同於德者德亦樂得之

同於失者失亦樂得之信不足焉有不信焉

企者不立跨者不行自見者不明

自是者不彰自伐者無功

自矜者不長其在道也曰

餘食贅行物或惡之故有道者不処

## TWENTY-FOUR

Those who stand on tiptoe are not steady.
Those who stride cannot maintain the pace.
Those who put on a show are not enlightened.
Those who are self-righteous are not respected.
Those who boast achieve nothing.
Those who brag will not endure.
According to followers of the Tao,
"These are unnecessary food and baggage."
They do not bring happiness.
Therefore followers of the Tao avoid them.

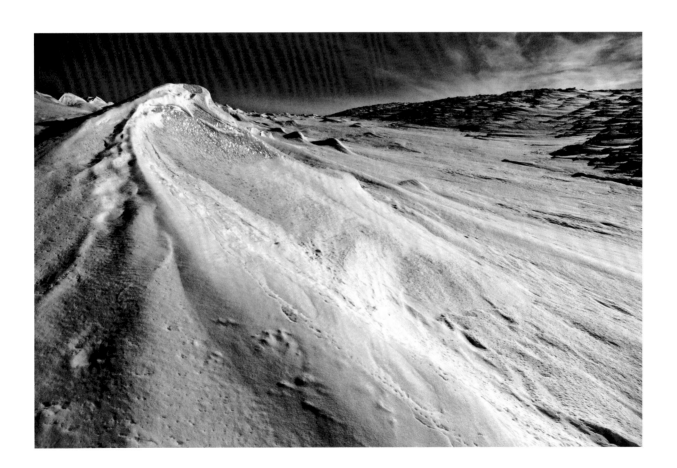

有物混成先天地生

寂兮寥兮獨立不改周行而不殆可以為天下母

吾不知其名字之曰道強為之名曰大

大曰逝逝曰遠遠曰反故道大天大地大王亦大

域中有四大而王居其一焉人法地地法天天法道道法自然

## Twenty-five

Something mysteriously formed,
Born before heaven and earth.
In the silence and the void,
Standing alone and unchanging,
Ever present and in motion.
Perhaps it is the mother of ten thousand things.
I do not know its name.
Call it Tao.
For lack of a better word, I call it great.

Being great, it flows.
It flows far away.
Having gone far, it returns.

Therefore, "Tao is great;
Heaven is great;
Earth is great;
The human being is also great."
These are the four great powers of the universe,
And the human being is one of them.

The human being follows the earth.
Earth follows heaven.
Heaven follows the Tao.
Tao follows what is natural.

Twenty-six

The heavy is the root of the light;
The still is the master of unrest.

Therefore the wise, traveling all day,
Do not lose sight of their baggage.
Though there are beautiful things to be seen,
They remain unattached and calm.

Why should the lord of ten thousand chariots act lightly in public?
To be light is to lose our root.
To be restless is to lose control.

重為輕根靜為躁君
是以聖人終日行不離輜重雖有榮觀燕處超然
奈何萬乘之主而以身輕天下輕則失本躁則失君

善行無轍迹善言無瑕讁善數不用籌策善閉無關楗而不可開善結無繩約而不可解

是以聖人常善救人故無棄人常善救物故無棄物

是謂襲明故善人者不善人之師不善人者善人之資不貴其師

不愛其資雖智大迷是謂要妙

TWENTY-SEVEN

A good walker leaves no tracks;
A good speaker makes no slips;
A good reckoner needs no tally.
A good door needs no lock,
Yet no one can open it.
Good binding requires no knots,
Yet no one can loosen it.

Therefore the wise take care of everyone
And abandon no one.
They take care of all things
And abandon nothing.

This is called "following the light."

What is a good person?
The teacher of a bad person.
What is a bad person?
A good person's charge.
If the teacher is not respected,
And the student not cared for,
Confusion will arise, however clever one is.
This is the crux of mystery.

知其雄守其雌為天下谿為天下谿常德不離復歸於嬰兒

知其白守其黑為天下式為天下式常德不忒復歸於無極

知其榮守其辱為天下谷為天下谷常德乃足復歸於樸

樸散則為器聖人用之則為官長故大制不割

Twenty-eight

Know the strength of a man,
But keep a woman's care!
Be the stream of the universe!
Being the stream of the universe,
Ever true and unswerving,
Become as a little child once more.

Know the white,
But keep the black!
Be an example to the world!
Being an example to the world,
Ever true and unwavering,
Return to the infinite.

Know honor,
Yet remain humble.
Be the valley of the universe!
Being the valley of the universe,
Ever true and resourceful,
Return to the state of the uncarved block.

When the block is carved, it becomes useful.
When the wise use it, they become rulers.
Thus, "A great tailor makes few cuts."

將欲取天下而為之吾見其不得已
天下神器不可為也為者敗之執者失之
故物或行或隨或歔或吹或強或羸或挫或隳
是以聖人去甚去奢去泰

Twenty-nine

Do you think you can conquer the universe and improve it?
I do not believe this can be done.

The universe is sacred.
You cannot improve it.
If you try to change it, you will ruin it.
If you try to hold on to it, you will lose it.

So sometimes things are ahead and sometimes they are behind;
Sometimes breathing is hard, sometimes it comes easily;
Sometimes there is strength, and sometimes weakness;
Sometimes one is up and sometimes down.

Therefore the wise avoid extremes, excesses, and complacency.

以道佐人主者不以兵強天下其事好還

師之所處荊棘生焉大軍之後必有凶年善有果而已不敢以取強

果而勿矜果而勿伐果而勿驕果而不得已果而勿強

物壯則老是謂不道不道早已

Thirty

Whenever you advise rulers in the way of Tao,
Counsel them not to use force to conquer the universe.
For this would only cause resistance.
Thorn bushes spring up wherever the army has passed.
Lean years follow in the wake of a great war.
Just do what needs to be done.
Never take advantage of power.

Achieve results,
But never glory in them.
Achieve results,
But never boast.
Achieve results,
But never be proud.
Achieve results,
Because this is the natural way.
Achieve results,
But not through violence.

Force is followed by loss of strength.
This is not the way of the Tao.
That which goes against the Tao
Comes to an early end.

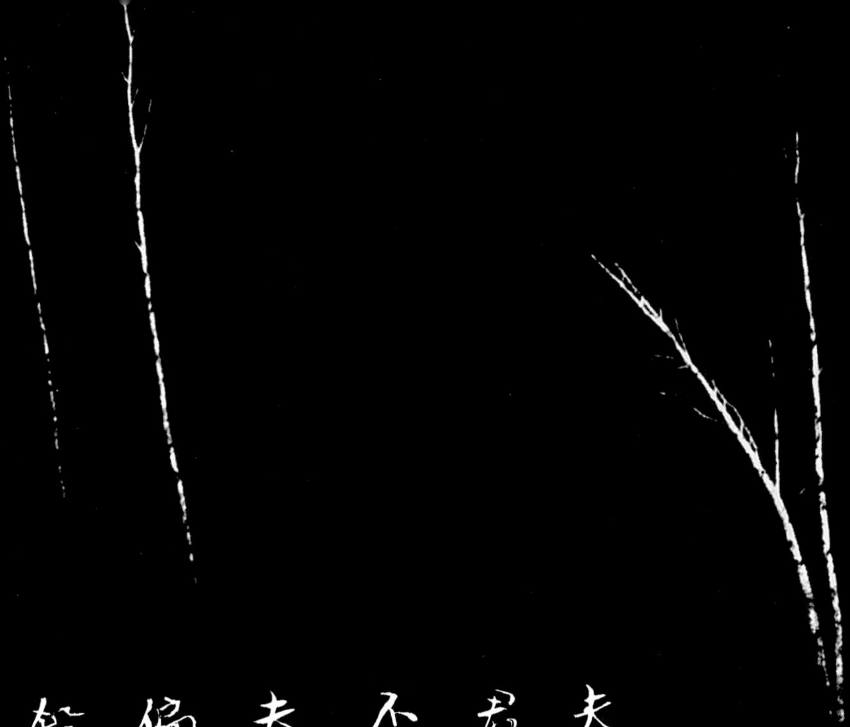

夫佳兵者不祥之器物或惡之故有道者不處

君子居則貴左用兵則貴右兵者不祥之器非君子之器

不得已而用之恬淡為上勝而不美而美之者是樂殺人

夫樂殺人者則不可以得志於天下矣吉事尚左凶事尚右

偏將軍居左上將軍居右言以喪禮處之

殺人之眾以哀悲泣之戰勝以喪禮處之

## Thirty-one

Good weapons are instruments of fear; all creatures hate them.
Therefore followers of Tao never use them.
The wise prefer the left.
Soldiers prefer the right.

Weapons are instruments of fear; they are not tools of the wise.
They use them only when there is no choice.
Peace and quiet are dear to their hearts,
And victory no cause for rejoicing.
If you rejoice in victory, then you delight in killing;
If you delight in killing, you cannot fulfill yourself.

On happy occasions precedence is given to the left,
On sad occasions to the right.
In the army the general stands on the left,
The commander-in-chief on the right.
This means that war is conducted like a funeral.
When many people are killed,
They should be mourned in heartfelt sorrow.
That is why a victory must be observed like a funeral.

道常無名樸雖小天下莫能臣也侯王君能守之萬物將自賓

天地相合以降甘露民莫之令而自均

始制有名名亦既有夫亦將知止知止可以不殆

辟言道之在天下猶川谷之於江海

## Thirty-two

The Tao is forever undefined.
Small though it is in the unformed state, it cannot be grasped.
If leaders could harness it,
The ten thousand things would naturally obey.
Heaven and earth would come together
And gentle rain fall.
People would no longer need laws and all things would take their course.

Once the whole is divided, the parts need names.
There are already enough names.
We need to know when to stop.
Knowing when to stop averts trouble.
Tao in the world is like a river flowing home to the sea.

知人者智　自知者明　勝人者有力　自勝者強
知足者富　強行者有志　不失其所者久　死而不亡者壽

## Thirty-three

Knowing others is wisdom;
Knowing the self is enlightenment.
Mastering others requires force;
Mastering the self needs strength.

Those who know they have enough are rich.
Perseverance is a sign of willpower.
Those who stay where they are endure.
To die but not to perish is to be eternally present.

## Thirty-four

The great Tao flows everywhere, both to the left and to the right.
The ten thousand things depend on it; it holds nothing back.
It fulfills its purpose silently and makes no claim.

It nourishes the ten thousand things,
But does not rule them.
It has no aim; it is very small.

The ten thousand things return to it,
Yet it does not rule them.
It is very great.

It does not show greatness,
And is therefore truly great.

執大象，天下往。往而不害，安平太。樂與餌，過客止。道之出口，淡乎其無味，視之不足見，聽之不足聞，用之不足既。

## Thirty-five

Everyone is drawn to those who keep to the one,
For there lie rest and happiness and peace.

Passersby may stop for music and good food,
But it is not possible to describe the Tao.
Without substance or flavor,
It cannot be seen, it cannot be heard,
And yet it cannot be exhausted.

Thirty-six

That which shrinks
Must first expand.
That which fails
Must first be strong.
That which is cast down
Must first be raised.
Before receiving
There must be giving.

This is called perception of the nature of things.
Soft and weak overcome hard and strong.

Fish cannot leave deep water,
And a country's weapons should not be displayed.

將欲歙之必固張之將欲弱之必固強之

將欲廢之必固興之將欲奪之必固與之

是謂微明柔弱勝剛強魚不可脫於淵

國之利器不可以示人

道常無為而無不為侯王若能守之

萬物將自化化而欲作吾將鎮之以無名之樸

無名之樸夫亦將無欲不欲以靜天下將自定之

THIRTY-SEVEN

Tao abides in non-action,
Yet nothing is left undone.
If those in power observed this,
The ten thousand things would develop naturally.
If they still desired to act,
They would return to the simplicity of formless substance.
Without form there is no desire.
Without desire there is tranquillity.
And in this way all things would be at peace.

上德不德是以有德下德不失德是以無德

上德無為而無以為下德為之而有以為

上仁為之而無以為上義為之而有以為上禮為之而莫之應則攘臂而扔之

故失道而後德失德而後仁失仁而後義失義而後禮夫禮者忠信之薄而亂之首

前識者道之華而愚之始是以大丈夫處其厚不居其薄處其實不居其華

故去彼取此

Thirty-eight

Truly good people are not aware of their goodness,
And are therefore good.
Foolish people try to be good,
And are therefore not good.

Truly good people do nothing,
Yet leave nothing undone.
Foolish people are always doing,
Yet much remains to be done.

When truly kind people do something, they leave nothing undone.
When just people do something, they leave a great deal to be done.
When disciplinarians do something and no one responds,
They roll up their sleeves and try to enforce order.

Therefore when Tao is lost, there is goodness.
When goodness is lost, there is kindness.
When kindness is lost, there is justice.
When justice is lost, there is ritual.
Now ritual is the husk of faith and loyalty, the beginning of confusion.
Knowledge of the future is only a flowery trapping of Tao.
It is the beginning of folly.

Therefore truly great people dwell on what is real and not what is on the surface,
On the fruit and not the flower.
Therefore accept the one and reject the other.

昔之得一者天得一以清地得一以寧神得一以靈谷得一以盈萬物得一以生侯王得一以為天下貞

其致之天無以清將恐裂地無以寧將恐發神無以靈將恐歇谷無以盈將恐竭

萬物無以生將恐滅侯王無以貴高將恐蹶故貴以賤為本高以下為基

是以侯王自謂孤寡不穀此非以賤為本邪非乎故致數輿無輿不欲琭琭如玉珞珞如石

## THIRTY-NINE

These things from ancient times arise from one:
The sky is whole and clear.
The earth is whole and firm.
The spirit is whole and strong.
The valley is whole and full.
The ten thousand things are whole and alive.
Those in power are whole, and the country is upright.
All these are in virtue of wholeness.

The clarity of the sky prevents it from falling.
The firmness of the earth prevents it from splitting.
The strength of the spirit prevents it from being exhausted.
The fullness of the valley prevents it from drying up.
The growth of the ten thousand things prevents their extinction.
Good leadership by those in power prevents the country from failing.

Therefore the humble is the root of the noble.
The low is the foundation of the high.
The wise consider themselves "orphaned," "widowed," and "worthless."
Their humility is the source of their strength.

Too much success is not an advantage.
Do not tinkle like jade
Or clatter like stone chimes.

反者道之動弱者道之用

天下萬物生於有有生於無

FORTY

Returning is the motion of the Tao.
Yielding is the way of the Tao.
The ten thousand things arise from being.
Being arises from not being.

Forty-one

The wise student hears of the Tao and practices it diligently.
The average student hears of the Tao and thinks about it now and then.
The foolish student hears of the Tao and laughs out loud
If there were no laughter, the Tao would not be what it is.

Hence it is said:
The bright path seems dim;
Going forward seems like retreat;
The easy way seems hard;
The highest Virtue seems empty;
Great purity seems sullied;
A wealth of Virtue seems inadequate;
The strength of Virtue seems frail;
Real Virtue seems unreal;
The perfect square has no corners;
Great talents ripen late;
The highest notes are hard to hear;
The greatest form has no shape.
The Tao is hidden and without name.
The Tao alone nourishes
And brings everything to fulfillment.

上士聞道勤而行之中士聞道若存若亡下士聞道大笑之不笑不足以為道

故建言有之明道若昧進道若退夷道若纇上德若谷

大白若辱廣德若不足建德若偷質真若渝

大方無隅大器晚成大音希聲大象無形

道隱無名夫唯道善貸且成

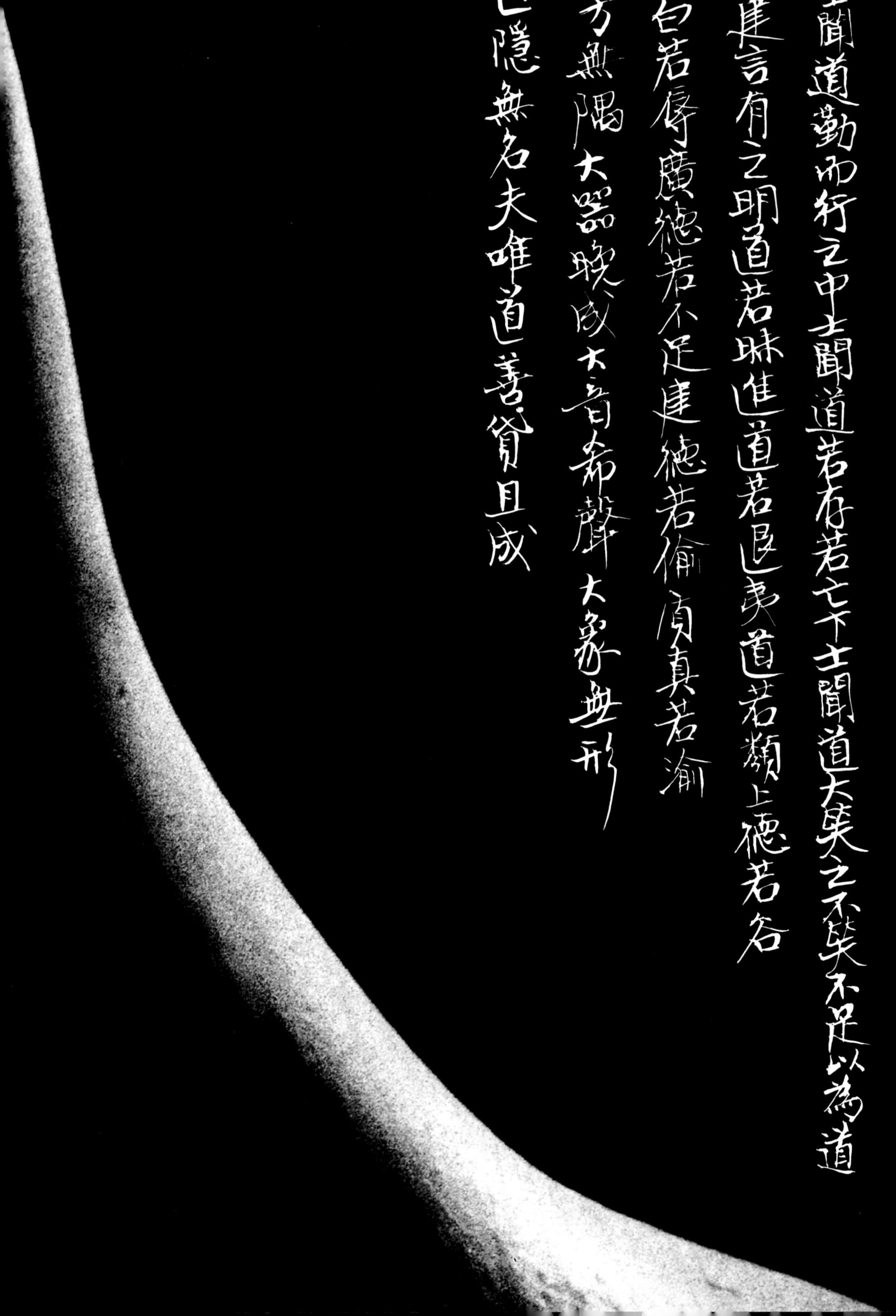

FORTY-TWO

The Tao begot one.
One begot two.
Two begot three.
And three begot the ten thousand things.

The ten thousand things carry yin and embrace yang.
They achieve harmony by combining these forces.

People hate to be "orphaned," "widowed," or "worthless,"
But this is how the wise describe themselves.

For one gains by losing
And loses by gaining.

What others teach, I also teach; that is:
"A violent person will die a violent death!"
This is the essence of my teaching.

道生一，一生二，二生三，三生萬物。萬物負陰而抱陽，沖氣以為和。

人之所惡，唯孤寡不穀，而王公以為稱。故物或損之而益，或益之而損。

人之所教，我亦教之。強梁者不得其死，吾將以為教父。

FORTY-THREE

The softest thing in the universe
Overcomes the hardest thing in the universe.
That without substance can enter where there is no room.
Hence I know the value of non-action.

Teaching without words and working without doing
Are understood by very few.

天下之至柔馳騁天下之至堅無有入無間

吾是以知無為之有益

不言之教無為之益天下希及之

名與身孰親身與貨孰多得與亡孰病
是故甚愛必大費多藏必厚亡
知足不辱知止不殆可以長久

Forty-four

Fame or self: Which matters more?
Self or wealth: Which is more precious?
Gain or loss: Which causes more pain?

Those who are attached to things will suffer greatly.
Those who save will suffer heavy losses.
Those who are contented are never disappointed.
Those who know when to stop do not find themselves in trouble.
They remain forever safe.

大成若缺其用不弊大盈若沖其用不窮

大直若屈大巧若拙大辯若訥

躁勝寒靜勝熱清靜為天下正

FORTY-FIVE

Great accomplishment seems imperfect,
Yet it does not outlive its usefulness.
Great fullness seems empty,
Yet it cannot be exhausted.

Great straightness seems twisted.
Great intelligence seems stupid.
Great eloquence seems awkward.

Movement overcomes cold.
Stillness overcomes heat.
Stillness and tranquillity restore order in the universe.

天下有道卻走馬以糞天下無道戎馬生於郊

禍莫大于不知足咎莫大于欲得故知足之足常足矣

FORTY-SIX

When the Tao is present in the universe,
The horses haul manure.
When the Tao is absent from the universe,
War horses are bred outside the city.

There is no greater sin than craving,
No greater curse than discontent,
No greater misfortune than wanting something for ourselves.
Therefore those who know that enough is enough will always have enough.

不出戶知天下不闚牖見天道其出彌遠其知彌少

是以聖人不行而知不見而名不為而成

Forty-seven

Without going outside, you may know the whole world.
Without looking through the window, you may see the ways of heaven.
The farther you go, the less you know.

Thus the wise know without traveling;
See without looking;
Work without doing.

為學日益為道日損

損之又損以至於無為無為而無不為

取天下常以無事及其有事不足以取天下

FORTY-EIGHT

In the pursuit of learning, something is acquired every day.
In the pursuit of the Tao, every day something is relinquished.

Less and less is done
Until non-action is achieved.
When nothing is done, nothing is left undone.

The world is governed by letting things take their course.
It cannot be governed through interference.

聖人無常心以百姓心為心善者吾善之

不善者吾亦善之德善者信者吾信之不信者吾亦信之德信

聖人在天下歙歙為天下渾其心百姓皆注其耳目聖人皆孩之

FORTY-NINE

The wise do not hold opinions.
They are aware of the needs of others.

I am good to people who are good.
I am also good to people who are not good,
Because Virtue is goodness.
I have faith in people who are faithful.
I also have faith in people who are not faithful,
Because Virtue is faithfulness.

The wise are shy and humble.
They behave like small children.
To the world they seem confusing.
Yet people look to them and listen.

出生入死生之徒十有三死之徒十有三人之生動之死地亦十有三夫何故以生生之厚

蓋聞善攝生者陸行不遇兕虎入軍不被甲兵

兕無所投其角虎無所措其爪兵無所容其刃

夫何故以其無死地

FIFTY

Between birth and death,
Three in ten are followers of life,
Three in ten are followers of death,
And people just passing from birth to death also number three in ten.
Why is this?
Because they live their lives on the gross level.

Those who know how to live walk abroad
Without fear of rhinoceroses or tigers.
They will not be wounded in battle.
For in them the rhinoceros finds no place to thrust its horn,
Nor the tiger to use its claws,
And weapons no place to pierce.
Why is this?
Because they have no place for death to enter.

道生之德畜之物形之勢成之

是以万物莫不尊道而貴德

道之尊德之貴夫莫之命而常自然

故道生之德畜之長之育之亭之毒之養之覆之

生而不有為而不恃長而不宰是謂元德

## FIFTY-ONE

All things arise from Tao.
They are nourished by Virtue.
They are formed from matter.
They are shaped by environment.
Thus the ten thousand things respect Tao and honor Virtue.
Respect of Tao and honor of Virtue are not demanded,
But they are in the nature of things.

Therefore all things arise from Tao.
By Virtue they are nourished,
Developed, cared for,
Sheltered, comforted,
Grown, and protected.
Creating without claiming,
Doing without taking credit,
Guiding without interfering.
This is Primal Virtue.

Fifty-two

The beginning of the universe
Is the mother of all things.
Knowing the mother, you also know the sons.
Knowing the sons, yet remaining in touch with the mother,
Brings freedom from the fear of death.

Keep your mouth shut,
Guard the senses,
And life is always full.
Open your mouth,
Always be busy,
And life is beyond hope.

Seeing the small is insight;
Yielding to force is strength.
Using the outer light, return to insight,
And in this way be saved from harm.
This is learning constancy.

天下有始以為天下母既知其母以知其子既知其子復守其母
沒身不殆塞其兌閉其門終身不勤開其兌濟其事終身不救
見小曰明守柔曰強用其光復歸其明無遺身殃是為習常

使我介然有知行於大道唯施是畏

大道甚夷而民好徑

朝甚除田甚蕪倉甚虛服文綵帶利劍厭飲食

財貨有餘是謂盜夸非道也哉

FIFTY-THREE

If I have even just a little sense,
I will walk on the main road and my only fear will be of straying from it.
Keeping to the main road is simple,
But people are easily distracted.

When the court is arrayed in splendor,
The fields are full of weeds,
And the granaries are empty.
Some wear gorgeous clothes,
Carry sharp swords,
And indulge in food and drink;
They have more possessions than they can use.
They are robber barons.
This is certainly not the way of Tao.

Fifty-four

What is firmly established cannot be uprooted.
What is firmly grasped cannot slip away.
It will be honored from generation to generation.

Cultivate Virtue in yourself,
And Virtue will be real.
Cultivate it in the family,
And Virtue will abound.
Cultivate it in the village,
And Virtue will grow.
Cultivate it in the nation,
And Virtue will be abundant.
Cultivate it in the universe,
And Virtue will be everywhere.

Therefore look at the body as body;
Look at the family as family;
Look at the village as village;
Look at the nation as nation;
Look at the universe as universe.

How do I know the universe is like this?
By looking!

善建者不拔善抱者不脱子孫以祭祀不輟

修之於身其德乃真修之於家其德乃餘

修之於鄉其德乃長修之於國其德乃豐

修之於天下其德乃普

故以身觀身以家觀家以鄉觀鄉以國觀國

以天下觀天下

吾何以知天下然哉以此

含德之厚比於赤子蜂蠆虺蛇不螫猛獸不據攫鳥不搏骨弱筋柔而握固
未知牝牡之合而全作精之至也終日号而不嗄 和之至也
知和曰常知常曰明 益生曰祥 心使气曰強物壯則老謂之不道不道早巳

Fifty-five

If you are filled with Virtue you are like a newborn child.
Wasps and serpents will not harm you;
Wild beasts will not pounce on you;
You will not be attacked by birds of prey.
Your bones are soft, your muscles weak,
But your grip is firm.
You have not experienced the union of man and woman, yet you are whole.
You are strong.
You may shout all day without becoming hoarse.
This is perfect harmony.

Knowing harmony is constancy.
Knowing constancy is enlightenment.

It is not wise to rush about.
Trying to control the breath causes strain.
If too much energy is used, exhaustion follows.
This is not the way of Tao.
Whatever is contrary to Tao will not last long.

知者不言言者不知塞其兌閉其門
挫其銳解其分和其光同其塵
是謂之同
故不可得而親亦不可得而疏
不可得而利亦不可得而害
不可得而貴亦不可得而賤
故為天下貴

Fifty-six

Those who know do not talk.
Those who talk do not know.

Close your mouth.
Guard your senses.
Temper your sharpness.
Simplify your problems.
Mask your brightness.
Be at one with the dust of the earth.
This is primal union.

Those who have achieved this state
Do not distinguish between friends and enemies,
Between good and harm, between honor and disgrace.
This is the highest state of being.

以正治國以奇用兵以無事取天下

吾何以知其然哉以此

天下多忌諱而民彌貧民多利器國家滋昏

人多伎巧奇物滋起法令滋彰盜賊多有

故聖人云我無為而民自化我好靜而民自正

我無事而民自富我無欲而民自樸

Fifty-seven

Rule a nation with justice.
Wage war with surprise tactics.
Become the master of the universe without striving.
How do I know that this is so?
Because of this!

The more laws and restrictions there are,
The poorer people become.
The sharper men's weapons,
The more trouble in the land.
The more ingenious and clever people are,
The more strange things happen.
The more rules and regulations,
The more thieves and robbers.

Therefore the wise one says:
"I take no action and people behave themselves.
I enjoy peace and people become honest.
I do nothing and people become rich.
I have no desires and people return to the good and simple life."

其政悶悶其政寥寥其民缺缺
禍兮福之所倚福兮禍之所伏孰知其極正
正復為奇善復為妖人之迷其日固久
是以聖人方而不割廉而不劌直而不肆光而不耀

FIFTY-EIGHT

When the country is ruled with a light hand
The people are simple.
When the country is ruled harshly,
The people are cunning.

Happiness is rooted in misery.
Misery lurks beneath happiness.
Who knows what the future holds?
There is no honesty.
Honesty becomes dishonest.
Goodness becomes delusion.
People's delusion lasts for a long time.

Therefore the wise are sharp but not cutting,
Pointed but not piercing,
Straightforward but not unrestrained,
Brilliant but not blinding.

治人事天莫若嗇 夫唯嗇 是謂早服 早服謂之重積德 重積德則無不克 無不克則莫知其極 莫知其極可以有國 有國之母可以長久 是謂深根固柢 長生久視之道

Fifty-nine

In caring for others and serving heaven,
There is nothing like using restraint.
Restraint begins with giving up our own ideas.
This depends on Virtue gathered in the past.
If there is a good store of Virtue, then nothing is impossible.
If nothing is impossible, then there are no limits.
If we know no limits, then we are fit to rule.
The mother principle of ruling holds good for a long time.
This is called having deep roots and a firm foundation,
The Tao of long life and eternal vision.

治大國若烹小鮮以道蒞天下其鬼不神非其鬼不神
其神不傷人非其神不傷人聖人亦不傷人
夫兩不相傷故德交歸焉

SIXTY

Ruling the country is like cooking a small fish.
Approach the universe with Tao,
And evil will have no power.
Not that evil is not powerful,
But its power will not be used to harm others.
Not only will it do no harm to others,
But the wise will also be protected.
We will not hurt one another,
And the Virtue in each of us refreshes everyone.

大國者下流，天下之交，天下之牝。

牝常以靜勝牡，以靜為下。

故大國以下小國，則取小國；小國以下大國，則取大國。故或下以取，或下而取。

大國不過欲兼畜人，小國不過欲入事人。

夫兩者各得所欲，大者宜為下。

Sixty-one

A great nation is like low land.
It is the meeting ground of the universe,
The mother of the universe.

The female overcomes the male with stillness,
Lying low in stillness.

Therefore if a great nation yields to a smaller nation,
It will conquer the smaller nation.
And if a smaller nation submits to a great nation,
It can conquer the great nation.
Therefore those who would conquer must yield,
And those who conquer do so through yielding.

A great nation needs more people;
A small nation needs to serve.
Each gets what it wants.
It is fitting for a great nation to yield.

SIXTY-TWO

Tao is the source of the ten thousand things.
It is the treasure of the good and the refuge of the bad.
Sweet words can buy honor;
Good deeds can gain respect.
If people are bad, do not abandon them.
Therefore on the day the emperor is crowned,
Or the three officers of state installed,
Do not send a gift of jade and a team of horses,
But remain still and offer the Tao.
Why does everyone value the Tao so much?
Isn't it because you find what you seek and are forgiven when you sin?
Therefore this is the greatest treasure in the universe.

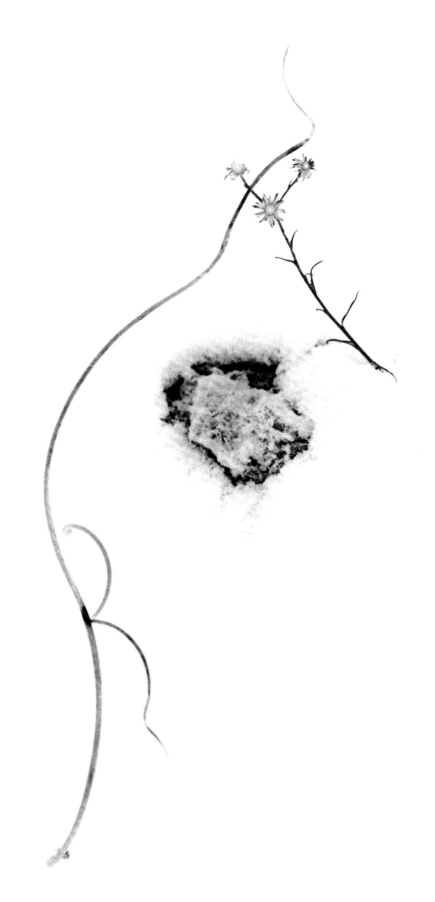

道者万物之奥善人之宝不善人之所保
美言可以市尊美行可以加人人之不善何棄之有
故立天子置三公雖有拱璧以先駟馬不如坐進此道
古之所以貴此道者何不曰求以得有罪以免邪故為天下貴

为无为，事无事，味无味。大小多少，报怨以德。
图难于其易，为大于其细。天下难事，必作于易；天下大事，必作于细。
是以圣人终不为大，故能成其大。
夫轻诺必寡信，多易必多难。
是以圣人犹难之，故终无难矣。

Sixty-three

Practice non-action.
Work without doing.
Taste the tasteless.
Magnify the small, increase the few.
Reward bitterness with care.

See simplicity in the complicated.
Achieve greatness in small things.

In the universe the difficult things are done as though they were easy.
In the universe great acts are made up of small deeds.
The wise do not attempt anything very big,
And thus achieve greatness.

Easy promises make for little trust.
Taking things lightly results in great difficulty.
Because the wise always confront difficulties,
They never experience them.

夫安易持其未兆易谋其脆易泮其微易散也治之于未有也治之于未乱

合抱之木生于毫末九层之台起于累土千里之行始于足下

为者败之执者失之是以圣人无为而故无败无执故无失

此言淳之常于然成而败之慎终如始则无败也

是以圣人欲不欲不贵难得之货学不学复众人之所过

以辅万物之自然而不敢为也

Sixty-four

Peace is easily maintained;
Trouble is easily overcome before it starts.
The brittle is easily shattered;
The small is easily scattered.

Deal with things before they happen.
Put things in order before there is confusion.

A tree as great as a man's embrace springs from a small shoot;
A terrace nine stories high begins with a pile of earth;
A journey of a thousand miles starts under one's feet.

Those who act defeat their own purpose;
Those who grasp lose.
The wise do not act and so are not defeated.
They do not grasp and therefore do not lose.

People usually fail when they are on the verge of success.
So give as much care to the end as to the beginning;
Then there will be no failure.

Therefore the wise seek freedom from desire.
They do not collect precious things.
They learn not to hold on to ideas.
They bring people back to what they have lost.
They help the ten thousand things find their own nature,
Yet they refrain from action.

古之善為道者，非以明民，將以愚之。民之難治，以其智多。故以智治國，國之賊；不以智治國，國之福。知此兩者亦稽式。常知稽式，是謂玄德。玄德深矣，遠矣，與物反矣，然後乃至大順。

Sixty-five

In the beginning those who knew the Tao did not try to enlighten others,
But kept it hidden.
Why is it so hard to rule?
Because the people are so clever.
Rulers who try to use cleverness
Cheat the country.
Those who rule without cunning
Are a blessing to the land.
These are the two alternatives.
Understanding these is Primal Virtue.
Primal Virtue goes deep and far.
It leads all things back
Toward the great oneness.

江海所以能為百谷王者
以其善下之，故能為百谷王
是以欲上民，必以言下之；欲先民，必以身後之
是以聖人處上而民不重，處前而民不害
是以天下樂推而不厭，以其不爭，故天下莫能與之爭

Sixty-six

Why is the sea king of a hundred streams?
Because it lies below them.
Therefore it is the king of a hundred streams.

If you would guide the people, you must serve with humility.
If you would lead them, you must follow behind.
In this way when you rule, the people will not feel oppressed;
When you stand before them, they will not be harmed.
The whole world will support you and will not tire of you.

Because you do not compete,
You will not have competition.

天下皆謂我道大似不肖夫唯大故似不肖若肖久矣其細也夫
我有三寶持而保之一曰慈二曰儉三曰不敢為天下先
慈故能勇儉故能廣不敢為天下先故能成器長
今舍慈且勇舍儉且廣舍後且先死矣
夫慈以戰則勝以守則固天將救之以慈衛之

SIXTY-SEVEN

Everyone under heaven says that my Tao is great and beyond compare.
Because it is great, it seems different.
If it were not different, it would have vanished long ago.

I have three treasures which I hold and keep.
The first is mercy; the second is economy;
The third is daring not to be ahead of others.
From mercy comes courage; from economy comes generosity;
From humility comes leadership.

Nowadays people shun mercy but try to be brave;
They abandon economy but try to be generous;
They do not believe in humility but always try to be first.
This is certain death.

Mercy brings victory in battle and strength in defense.
It is the means by which heaven saves and guards.

## Sixty-eight

A good soldier is not violent.
A good fighter is not angry.
A good winner is not vengeful.
A good employer is humble.
This is known as the Virtue of not striving.
This is known as the ability to deal with people.
This since ancient times has been known as the ultimate unity with heaven.

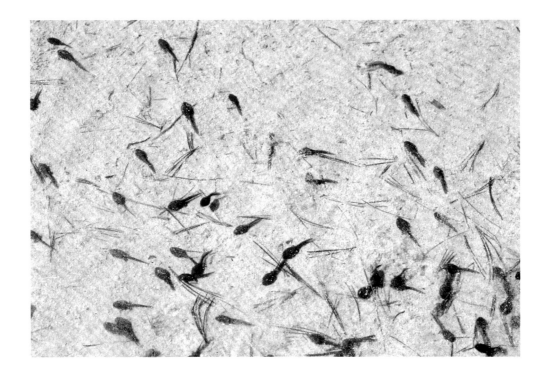

用兵有言吾不敢為主而為客不敢進寸而退尺
是謂行無行攘無臂扔無敵執無兵
禍莫大於輕敵輕敵幾喪吾寶故抗兵相加哀者勝矣

Sixty-nine

There is a saying among soldiers:
"I dare not make the first move but would rather play the guest;
I dare not advance an inch but would rather withdraw a foot."

This is called marching without appearing to move,
Rolling up your sleeves without showing your arm,
Capturing the enemy without attacking,
Being armed without weapons.

There is no greater catastrophe than underestimating the enemy.
By underestimating the enemy, I risk losing what I value.

Therefore when the battle is joined,
The underdog will win.

SEVENTY

My words are easy to understand and easy to perform,
Yet no one under heaven knows them or practices them

My words have ancient beginnings.
My actions are disciplined.
Because people do not understand, they have no knowledge of me.

Those that know me are few;
Those that abuse me are honored.
Therefore the wise wear rough clothing and hold the jewel in their heart.

吾言甚易知甚易行天下莫能知莫能行
言有宗事有君夫唯無知是以不我知
知我者希則我者貴是以聖人被褐懷玉

SEVENTY-ONE

Knowing ignorance is strength.
Ignoring knowledge is sickness.

If one is sick of sickness, then one is not sick.
The wise are not sick because they are sick of sickness.
Therefore they are not sick.

知不知上不知知病夫唯病病是以不病聖人不病以其病病是以不病

民不畏威則大威至
無狎其所居無厭其所生夫唯不厭是以不厭
是以聖人自知不自見自愛不自貴故去彼取此

SEVENTY-TWO

When people lack a sense of awe, there will be disaster.

Do not intrude into their homes.
Do not harass them at work.
If you do not interfere, they will not weary of you.

Therefore the wise know themselves but make no show,
Have self-respect but are not arrogant.
They let go of that and choose this.

勇於敢則殺勇於不敢則活此兩者或利或害
天之所惡孰知其故是以聖人猶難之
天之道不爭而善勝不言而善應不召而自來
繟然而善謀天網恢恢疏而不失

SEVENTY-THREE

A brave and passionate person will kill or be killed.
A brave and calm person will always preserve life.
Of these two which is good and which is harmful?
Some things are not favored by heaven. Who knows why?
Even the wise are unsure of this.

The Tao of heaven does not strive and yet it overcomes.
It does not speak and yet is answered.
It does not ask, yet all its needs are met.
It seems to have no aim and yet its purpose is fulfilled.

Heaven's net is cast wide.
Though its meshes are coarse, nothing slips through.

Seventy-four

If people are not afraid to die,
It is of no avail to threaten them with death.

If people live in constant fear of dying,
And if breaking the law means that someone will be killed,
Who will dare to break the law?

There is always an official executioner.
If you try to take his place,
It is like trying to be a master carpenter and cutting wood.
If you try to cut wood like a master carpenter, you will only hurt your hand.

民不畏死奈何以死懼之

若使民常畏死而為奇者吾得執而殺之孰敢

常有司殺者殺夫代司殺者殺是謂代大匠斲

夫代大匠斲者希有不傷其手矣

民之饑以其上食稅之多是以饑民之難治以其上之有為是以難治民之輕死以其上求生之厚是以輕死夫唯無以生為者是賢於貴生

SEVENTY-FIVE

Why are the people starving?
Because the rulers eat up the money in taxes.
Therefore the people are starving.

Why are the people rebellious?
Because the rulers interfere too much.
Therefore the people are rebellious.

Why do the people think so little of death?
Because the rulers demand too much of life.
Therefore the people take death lightly.

Having little to live on, they know better than to value life too highly.

人之生也柔弱其死也堅強萬物草木之生也柔脆

其死也枯槁故堅強者死之徒柔弱者生之徒

是以兵強則不勝木強則兵強大處下柔弱處上

## SEVENTY-SIX

We are born gentle and weak, but at death are stiff and hard.
Green plants are tender and filled with sap.
At their death they are withered and dry.

Therefore the stiff and unbending is the disciple of death.
The gentle and yielding is the disciple of life.

Thus an army without flexibility never wins a battle.
A tree that is unbending is easily broken.

The hard and strong will fall.
The soft and weak will overcome.

天之道其猶張弓與高者抑之下者舉之

有餘者損之不足者補之

天之道損有餘而補不足人之道則不然損不足以奉有餘

孰能有餘以奉天下唯有道者

是以聖人為而不恃功成而不處其不欲見賢

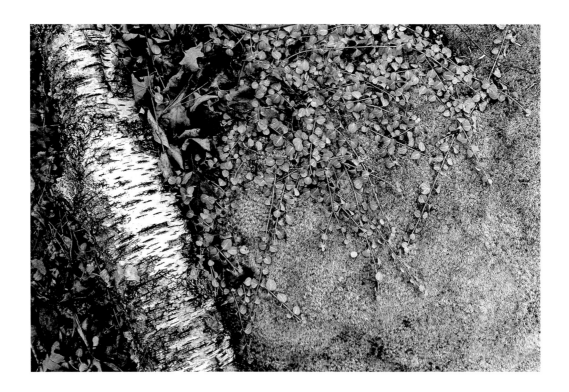

SEVENTY-SEVEN

The Tao of heaven is like bending a bow.
The high is lowered and the low is raised.
If the string is too long, it is shortened;
If there is not enough, it is made longer.

The Tao of heaven is to take from those who have too much and give to those who do not have enough.
Ordinary people act differently.
They take from those who do not have enough and give to those who already have too much.
Who has more than enough and gives it to the world?
Only the wise.

Therefore the wise work without recognition.
They achieve what has to be done without dwelling on it.
They do not try to show their knowledge.

天下莫柔弱於水　而攻堅強者莫之能勝　以其無以易之
弱之勝強　柔之勝剛　天下莫不知　莫能行
是以聖人云　受國之垢　是謂社稷主　受國不祥
是謂天下王　正言若反

## Seventy-eight

Under heaven nothing is more soft and yielding than water.
Yet for attacking the solid and strong, nothing is better;
It has no equal.
The weak can overcome the strong;
The supple can overcome the stiff.
Under heaven everyone knows this,
Yet no one puts it into practice.
Therefore the wise say:
"If you take on the humiliation of the people, you are fit to rule them.
If you take upon yourself the country's disasters,
You deserve to be ruler of the universe."
The truth often sounds paradoxical.

SEVENTY-NINE

After a bitter quarrel, some resentment remains.
What can be done about this?
The wise keep their half of the bargain
But do not exact their due.
Virtuous people perform their part,
But those without Virtue require others to fulfill their obligations.
The Tao of heaven is impartial.
It remains with those who are good.

和大怨必有餘怨安可以為善是以聖人執左契
而不責於人有德司契無德司徹天道無親常與善人

小國寡民使有什伯之器而不用

使民重死而不遠徙雖有舟輿無所乘之

雖有甲兵無所陳之使人復結繩而用之

甘其食美其服安其居乐其俗

鄰國相望雞犬之声相聞

民至老死不相往來

EIGHTY

A small country has fewer people.
Though there are machines that can work ten to a hundred times faster than people,
They are not needed.
The people take death seriously and do not travel far.
Though they have boats and carriages, no one uses them.
Though they have armor and weapons, no one displays them.
People return to the knotting of rope in place of writing.
Their food is plain and healthy, their clothes fine but simple, their homes secure;
They are happy in their lives.
Though they live within sight of their neighbors,
And crowing cocks and barking dogs are heard across the way,
Yet they leave each other in peace while they grow old and die.

信言不美美言不信善者不辯辯者不善知者不博博者不知

聖人不積既以為人己愈有既以與人己愈多

天之道利而不害聖人之道為而不爭

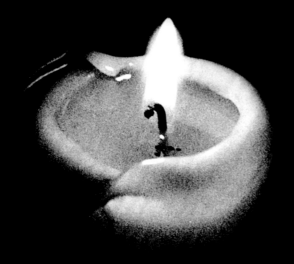

## EIGHTY-ONE

Truthful words are not beautiful.
Beautiful words are not truthful.
Good people do not argue.
Those who argue are not good.
Those who know are not learned.
The learned do not know.

The wise never try to hold onto things.
The more you do for others, the more you have.
The more you give to others, the greater your abundance.
The Tao of heaven is sharp but does no harm.
The Tao of the wise is to work without effort.

*A Rainbow of Tao.* This full-color book by Jane English is many things: a retrospective story of the author's fifty-year journey with Tao, a blossoming into color photography, an introduction to Tao for those who have not heard of it, an expanded understanding of Tao beyond things ancient and Chinese to its true nature, the fullness of all that is.
Available at www.eheart.com.

*Chuang Tsu: Inner Chapters.* A new edition of the companion to Gia-fu Feng and Jane English's translation of *Tao Te Ching,* with over one hundred photos, updated translation, and introduction by Chungliang Al Huang. Chuang Tsu anticipated Zen Buddhism's emphasis on a state of emptiness or ego transcendence. With humor, imagery, and fantasy, he captures the depth of Chinese thinking.
Available at www.hayhouse.com and at www.eheart.com.

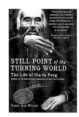

*Still Point of the Turning World: The Life of Gia-fu Feng.* An award-winning biography by Carol Ann Wilson. This book interweaves the life of translator, teacher, Taoist rogue Gia-fu Feng with the tumultuous historical tapestry of twentieth-century China and the United States. From Chinese warlords, Japanese occupation, and World War II to 1950s disillusionment, the Beats, Esalen, and beyond, it tracks a life that began with external privilege but culminated in the gradual discovery of the still point within. Available at www.carolannwilson.info and at www.eheart.com.

*Tao Calendar.* Now in full color, this annual wall calendar uses text and calligraphy from *Tao Te Ching* and *Chuang Tsu,* with new photographs by Jane English each year.
Available at www.amberlotus.com and at www.eheart.com.

---

JANE ENGLISH, whose photographs form an integral part of this book, was born in Boston, Massachusetts in 1942. She holds a BA from Mount Holyoke College and received her doctorate in experimental high energy particle physics from the University of Wisconsin–Madison in 1970. Her other books include *Different Doorway: Adventures of a Caesarean Born, Fingers Pointing to the Moon,* and *The Ceremony Cards.* Her current work may be seen at www.eheart.com.

GIA-FU FENG was born in 1919 in the ancient city of Suzhou. He grew up in Shanghai, where his father was one of the founders of the Bank of China. During World War II, he graduated from Peking University, part of National Southwestern Associated University, a university in exile in Kunming, Free China. He came to the United States in 1947 and earned a master's degree in international banking at the Wharton School. In meeting Alan Watts in San Francisco and studying at the American Academy of Asian Studies, he found the path he had been seeking. He taught at Esalen Institute in Big Sur, California, and founded Stillpoint Foundation, a Taoist community in California, then Colorado, where he lived until his death in 1985.

TOINETTE LIPPE began her publishing career in London and came to the United States in 1964. She worked at Alfred A. Knopf for more than thirty years as reprint rights director and senior editor. In 1989, while still at Knopf, she founded Bell Tower, where she edited seventy books that nourish the soul, illuminate the mind, and speak directly to the heart. Her own books *Nothing Left Over: A Plain and Simple Life* and *Caught in the Act: Reflections on Being, Knowing, and Doing* were published in 2002 and 2004, respectively. She now devotes herself to East Asian brush painting and her paintings and cards can be seen at www.toinettelippe.com.

JACOB NEEDLEMAN is professor emeritus of philosophy at San Francisco State University. He was educated at Harvard, Yale, and the University of Freiburg, Germany. He is the author of numerous books, including *Lost Christianity, The American Soul, Why Can't We Be Good?,* and *What Is God?.* In addition to his teaching and writing, he serves as a consultant in the fields of psychology, education, medical ethics, and philanthropy, and he was featured on Bill Moyers's acclaimed PBS series, *A World of Ideas.* www.jacobneedleman.com.

## Location, Date, and Medium Type of the Photographs

BW = black-and-white print     S = color slide
C = color print     D = digital

L = left
R = right

Title page    Twig on snow, location forgotten, c. 1996 (BW)

1 L   Hills near Garberville, Calif., 1970 (BW)
1 R   Sunrise over Green Bay, Door County, Wis., c. 1967 (BW)

2 L   Feather, 1987 (BW)
2 R   Big old hardwood tree near Dole, France, 2011 (D)

3 L   Ice in a small creek in southeast Oregon, 1990 (C)
3 R   Field and woods in Calais, Vt., 2005 (S)

4 L   Fog on Cannon Mountain, N.H., c. 1967 (BW)
4 R   Pond lily, Calais, Vt. 2007 (D)

5 L   Snow on Mt. Tamalpais, Marin County, Calif., 1982 (BW)
5 R   Old maple tree, Tamworth, N.H., c. 1970 (BW)

6 L   Shell found on a beach, Long Island, N.Y., 1968 (BW)
6 R   Burdock leaf and fern, Calais, Vt., 1971 (BW)

7 L   Clouds, New Hampshire, c. 1991 (S)
7 R   New leaves, New Hampshire, c. 2004 (C)

8 L   At Diana's Baths, North Conway, N.H., 2009 (D)
8 R   Sunset, Calais, Vt., 2003 (S)

9 L   Winter farmland, Calais, Vt., 2007 (D)
9 R   Rock in white pine bark, Chocorua, N.H., 1998 (S)

10 L   Mills Meadow near Mt. Shasta, Calif., 2001 (S)
10 R   Painted trillium, Calais, Vt., 2007 (D)

11 L   Sunset near Rochester, Vt., 2010 (D)
11 R   Frosty window, Wisconsin, c. 1967 (BW)

12 L   Yosemite National Park, Calif., 1970 (BW)
12 R   Oak leaf, Madison, Wis., c. 1966 (BW)

13 L   Fir snag, somewhere in California, c. 1971 (BW)
13 R   Lenticular cloud, Mt. Washington, N.H., 2010 (D)

14 L   Parfrey's Glen near Baraboo, Wis., 1967 (BW)
14 R   Dry grass, location forgotten, before 1978 (BW)

15 L   Frosty morning, Calais, Vt., 2007 (D)
15 R   Hardwood tree, Madison, Wis., c. 1966 (BW)

16 L   Moonrise over Mount Shasta, Calif., c. 1992 (S)
16 R   Springtime branches, Madison, Wis., c. 1967 (BW)

17 L   Sunrise, location forgotten, c. 1973 (BW)
17 R   Sugar pine and cumulus, near Mt. Shasta, Calif., 2002 (S)

18 L   Wave marks, location forgotten, before 1978 (BW)
18 R   Corner of Taliesin, Spring Green, Wis., c. 1967 (BW)

19 L   Copper beech, Mount Holyoke College, Mass., c. 1969 (S)
19 R   Mule deer near Tule Lake, Calif., 1999 (S)

20 L   Mt. Tamalpais, Calif., c. 1966 (BW)
20 R   Fern, Point Reyes, Calif., 1987 (BW)

21 L   Chocorua Lake and Mt. Chocorua, N.H., 1998 (C)
21 R   Mountain hemlock, Mt. Shasta, Calif., c. 1995 (S)

22 L   Reeds, Calais, Vt., 1971 (BW)
22 R   Mallow flowers, Calais, Vt., c. 2005 (D)

23 L   Tracks under birch branch, Calais, Vt., c. 2008 (D)
23 R   Winter sky and tree, Calais, Vt., 2003 (S)

24 L   Oak leaf in snow, Tamworth, N.H., c. 1982 (BW)
24 R   At the edge of the Big Ice, Greenland, 2010 (D)

25 L   Firs in fog, near Mt. Shasta, Calif., 1996 (BW)
25 R   Forest floor, near Taos, N.M., c. 1973 (BW)

26 L   Rock on beach, near Crescent City, Calif., 1992 (S)
26 R   White pine, Topsfield, Mass., c. 2003 (S)

27 L   Firs and maples, Livermore, N.H., 1976 (BW)
27 R   Diana's Baths, North Conway, N.H., 2009 (D)

28 L   White birch bark, Jackson, N.H., c. 1998 (C)
28 R   Shell found on a beach, Long Island, N.Y., 1968 (BW)

29 L   Santa Cruz Mountains, Calif., c. 1970 (BW)
29 R   Ferns and flower, Calais, Vt., 2004 (D)

30 L   Mouse tracks near Mt. Shasta, Calif., 1987 (BW)
30 R   Elm, Madison, Wis., c. 1966 (BW)

31 L   Birches in southern Wisconsin, c. 1966 (BW)
31 R   Bushes in snow, Topsfield, Mass., 1968 (BW)

32 L   Shore of Lake Michigan, Wis., c. 1967 (BW)
32 R   Beach grass near Lake Michigan, c. 1967 (BW)

33 L   Sugar pine and firs, near Mt. Shasta, Calif., c. 2000 (S)
33 R   Elm, Madison, Wis., c. 1966 (BW)

34 L   Big and small maple trees, Marshfield, Vt., 2007 (D)
34 R   Jane's cat, near Mt. Shasta, Calif., 2000 (S)

35 L   Snow-covered trees, Calais, Vt., 2007 (D)
35 R   Open door, Calais, Vt., 1971, (BW)

36 L   Old maple, Franconia Notch, N.H., 2004 (S)
36 R   Diana's Baths, North Conway, N.H., 2009 (D)

37 L   Ferns, Calais, Vt., 1971 (BW)
37 R   Sunset, Marin County, Calif., c. 1979 (BW)

38 L   White pine cone, Jackson, N.H., 1998 (C)
38 R   Near Cottonwood Pass, Colo., c. 1973 (BW)

39 L   Eucalyptus, Berkeley, Calif., 1965 (BW)
39 R   Young ferns, Calais, Vt., 2007 (D)

40 L  Cottonwood, Boulder, Colo., 2007 (D)
40 R  Bare aspen trees, Aspen, Colo., c. 1973 (S)

41 L  Lenticular clouds near Mt. Shasta, Calif., c. 1999 (S)
41 R  Closeup of shell (see 28R)

42 L  Reflected trees, Madison, Wis., c. 1966 (BW)
42 R  Crescent moon, near Mt. Shasta, Calif., c. 1999 (S)

43 L  Gia-fu walking in Yosemite National Park, 1970 (BW)
43 R  Yosemite National Park, Calif., 1970 (BW)

44 L  White pine, South Conway, N.H., 2007 (D)
44 R  Tree lace, Sandpoint, Idaho, 1984 (BW)

45 L  Maples, Tamworth, N.H., 1984 (BW)
45 R  Red cabbage in Jane's garden, Mt. Shasta, Calif., 1998 (S)

46 L  Mt. Willard, Crawford Notch, N.H., 2010 (D)
46 R  From Pine Mtn., near Mt. Washington, N.H., c. 1966 (BW)

47 L  Barn and clouds, Corinth, Vt., 2008 (D)
47 R  Tip-top House, Mt. Washington, N.H., 2007 (D)

48 L  Gull, Lake Michigan, c. 1967 (BW)
48 R  Dew on plants, San Francisco, Calif., 1981 (BW)

49 L  Doves in fir, Santa Cruz Mountains, Calif., 1971 (BW)
49 R  Mirror Lake, Calais, Vt., 2007 (D)

50 L  Aspen tree, Colorado, 1994 (C)
50 R  Beetle, Jackson, N.H., c. 1998 (C)

51 L  White birches, Calais, Vt., 2011 (D)
51 R  Tamarack tree in winter, Calais, Vt., 2007 (D)

52 L  Winter trees, Jackson, N.H., 1998 (C)
52 R  Sugar pine near Mt. Shasta, Calif., c. 2000 (S)

53 L  Cedars near Mt. Shasta, Calif., c. 2001 (S)
53 R  Ferns by roadside, Calais, Vt., 2005 (D)

54 L  Old stump, Wisconsin, c. 1965 (BW)
54 R  Mt. Tamalpais, Calif., c. 1966 (BW)

55 L  Birches and pines, Calais, Vt., 2007 (D)
55 R  Sun and clouds, Manitou Springs, Colo., c. 1973 (BW)

56 L  Wasatch Mountains, Utah, c. 1974 (BW)
56 R  Pikes Peak, Colo., c. 1973 (BW)

57 L  Crystal Lake, Eaton, N.H., 2007 (D)
57 R  White birches, Calais, Vt., 2007 (D)

58 L  Lake Umbagog, Me., c. 1973 (BW)
58 R  Seaweed on rock, Prince Edward Is., Canada, 1973 (BW)

59 L  Trees reflected, Calais, Vt., 2003 (S)
59 R  Frog in mud, near Mt. Shasta, Calif., 1999 (S)

60 L  Spiderweb, Calais, Vt., 1971 (BW)
60 R  Reflection in duck pond, Wisconsin, c. 1967 (BW)

61 L  Cloudy sky, Calais, Vt., c. 2007 (D)
61 R  Field and trees from Gibraltar Rock, Wis., c. 1966 (BW)

62 L  Woodpecker, Calais, Vt., 2008 (D)
62 R  Near Mineral Hot Springs, Colo., 1971 (BW)

63 L  Budding shrub, Madison, Wis., c. 1966 (BW)
63 R  Trees in autumn, Markesan, Wis. c. 1968 (BW)

64 L  Pines, White Mountains, New Hampshire, 2009 (D)
64 R  Ferns, Calais, Vt., 2007 (D)

65 L  Niagara Falls, Canada, 2009 (D)
65 R  Lake Mendota, Madison, Wis., c. 1968 (BW)

66 L  Big Sur, Calif., c. 1975 (BW)
66 R  Pikes Peak, Colo. c. 1972 (BW)

67 L  Maple branch, Tamworth, N.H., 1984 (BW)
67 R  Oak leaves in snow, Calais, Vt., c. 2003 (S)

68 L  Waterfall, Woodbury, Vt., 2007 (D)
68 R  Tadpoles near Mt. Shasta, Calif., c. 2001 (S)

69 L  White birches, Jackson, N.H., 1998 (C)
69 R  Beach, Door County, Wis., c. 1966 (BW)

70 L  Icy birch, location forgotten, c. 1966 (BW)
70 R  Mountainside, location forgotten, c. 1966 (BW)

71 L  Wasatch Mountains, Utah, c. 1974 (BW)
71 R  Striped maple leaves, Jackson, N.H., c. 1971 (BW)

72 L  Oaks and dead pine, Jackson, N.H., c. 1971 (BW)
72 R  Swallows on wires, New Hampshire, c. 1966 (BW)

73 L  Maidenhair fern, 1971 (photogram)
73 R  Fog, near Garberville, Calif., 1970 (BW)

74 L  Great Sand Dunes National Park, Colo., 2007 (D)
74 R  Gulls in Maine, c. 1973 (BW)

75 L and R   Parfrey's Glen, near Baraboo, Wis., 1967 (BW)

76 L  Sunset in Big Sur, Calif., 1983 (BW)
76 R  Parfrey's Glen, Wis., 1967 (BW)

77 L  Ferns, Jackson, N.H., 2007 (D)
77 R  Birch log, Jackson, N.H., c. 1984 (C)

78 L  Gull over Lake Huron, c. 1967 (BW)
78 R  Ipswich River, Topsfield, Mass., c. 1966 (BW)

79 L  Grass and rock, somewhere in Wisconsin, c. 1967 (BW)
79 R  Mt. Willard, Crawford Notch, N.H., 2007 (D)

80 L  Maple branch, Calais, Vt., 2007 (D)
80 R  Fritillary butterfly, Colorado, c. 1973 (S)

81 L and R   Candles, Madison, Wis., c. 1967 (BW)